ALSO BY JESSICA B. HARRIS

The Welcome Table:
African-American Heritage Cooking

Tasting Brazil:
Regional Recipes and Reminiscences

Sky Juice and Flying Fish:
Traditional Caribbean Cooking

Iron Pots and Wooden Spoons:
Africa's Gifts to New World Cooking

Hot Stuff:
A Cookbook in Praise of the Piquant

SIMON & SCHUSTER New York London Toronto Sydney Tokyo Singapore

CELEBRATING THE HOLIDAY

A KWANZAA KEEPSAKE

WITH NEW TRADITIONS AND FEASTS

JESSICA B. HARRIS

SIMON & SCHUSTER
Rockefeller Center
1230 Avenue of the Americas
New York, NY 10020

Designed by Barbara Marks

Manufactured in the United States of America

1 3 5 7 9 10 8 6 4 2

Library of Congress Cataloging-in-Publication Data
Harris, Jessica B.
A Kwanzaa keepsake : celebrating the holiday with new traditions
and feasts / Jessica B. Harris.
p.   cm.
Includes index.
1. Kwanzaa.   2. Afro-Americans—Social life and customs.   3. Afro-
American cookery.   4. United States—Social life and customs.
I. Title.
GT4403.H37   1995   95-4943
394.2'61—dc20   CIP

ISBN: 0-684-80045-4

ACKNOWLEDGMENTS

First thanks must be given to Maulana Karenga. Had he not seen the need for Kwanzaa thirty years ago, we would not have this magnificent holiday that gives us as a people a time for reflection, renewal, and rebirth.

Thanks then go to all of those who went before who brought us to the point where we can celebrate our strengths and heal our differences.

I want to particularly thank Marcella Martinez, Mary Brennan, and my pit bull researcher "daughter," Patricia D. Hopkins, who helped nail down dates, check spellings, and find out if folks still walked the earth.

Thanks are due to the support team who come, eat, and encourage. They know who they are and I thank them from the bottom of my heart, the bottoms of my cooking pots, and the bottoms of the plates that they invariably clean. Thanks particularly to Robert, June, and Kamau Bobb, Charlayne Hunter-Gault and the Vineyard crew, Ayo Fenner, Pat Lawrence, Johnny Rivers, Clayton Sherrod, Charlotte Lyons, all of Rabbit's friends and relations, and my "bay at the moon" friends, particularly those who come from as far away as Brazil and as near as around the block each year to my Kwanzaa/New Year's bash.

To my new friends around the country who encourage and support, and to my international family including Theophile and Theodora Komaclo, who are finally in the same town with me, and the rest of my West African family including Aimée and Albert Grimaud, Léonie, Suzanne, and others too numerous to name. To Maryse Pochot, and her children, Bruce and Jennifer, as well as Maman Guadeloupe, my "new brothers and sisters-in-law," Sonny and Aubert Tancons, Janine, Serge, 'TiKa, and my whole new family there. To Norma Shirley, Maria Williams-Jones, and Asif Williams and Edwin Jones in Jamaica, to Patricia Wilson and the crew at Bistro Gambaro in Puerto Rico, and the one whose name I left out. . . . You know who you are.

My spiritual lifeline of the filhas at Casa Branca in Brazil, particularly minha Mae Tata, Zurika, Kutu, Tereza, Celina, Terezinha, Mariana, Tieta, Morena, Sinha and her children, and my secular Brazilian family Marcelo, Guilherme, and Alba Figuereido, Vera Dodebei, Haroldo and Maria Costa in Rio, and Antonio Luis Figuereido, Tereza, Bianca, Pablo, and the rest of the family in Bahia.

My personal thanks go to my editor, Sydny Miner, who always seems to understand what I mean even when I haven't said it, and her able assistant, Erin Cartwright.

To my agent, Carole, who had faith in me before any others.

Thanks must also go to Ron Cottman, who is always willing to go beyond his job helping me restore my very old house, and give me a hand with cleaning stoves, babysitting cats, and otherwise keeping my life in running order.

Finally there are not enough thanks to go to my mother, without whom I would get nothing written. At eighty-two, she puts up with my questions, tests recipes, and just keeps me going. I pray nightly her energy is genetic.

Kwanzaa ends with *Imani* (faith), so I too must end my acknowledgments by thanking the Creative Spirit. Without guidance from divine hands nothing I do would get done.

—Aṣẹ

I celebrated my first Kwanzaa in the home of friends in Bedford Stuyvesant, Brooklyn, in New York City. The celebration was small and the three younger children in the family were thrilled to be participating in the ceremony. The son, a bright young child, eyes gleaming with thoughts of the holiday, lit the candle and spoke briefly yet movingly about the *Kujichagulia*—self-determination. I was moved, and vowed to celebrate the holiday in my own small way even though I have no children of my own.

As I write this, that bright young child of ten years ago is dead, killed by random street violence. *A Kwanzaa Keepsake* is for his memory and for African-American children and parents everywhere. May the principles of Kwanzaa reinforce the values of our families and keep all of our children, those of the womb and those of the heart, safe.

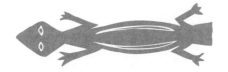

CONTENTS

WHAT IS KWANZAA?

Those who think that holidays are days steeped in centuries-old tradition are always surprised to hear that the African-American feast of Kwanzaa was established in 1966. That was the year Maulana Karenga decided that African-Americans needed a time of cultural reaffirmation. He looked east to Africa, East Africa, and came up with a celebration that is a compilation of several harvest festivals and celebrations that are held throughout the continent. The name *Kwanzaa* comes from the Swahili word *kwanza,* meaning "first," as in the phrase *matunda ya kwanza* (first fruits). The second "a" distinguishes the African-American from the African *kwanza.* An apocryphal tale is told that during one of the early Kwanzaa celebrations, a children's pageant was held, with each child holding up a card with the letters of the word *kwanza,* which at that time was spelled with one "a." One child was left, letterless and weeping, at the end of the row. A second "a" was quickly produced, the day was saved, and the holiday was forever after known as Kwanzaa.

Occurring annually from December 26 to January 1, Kwanzaa is a time of fasting, of feasting, and of self-examination. It was at first celebrated mainly by cultural nationalists who wished to express their Pan-African solidarity. Yet, as word of the new holiday and its family-strengthening virtues spread, African-Americans from all walks of life began to celebrate the seven nights of reflection. Today, over 13 million people of all political leanings and in all walks of life celebrate the holiday, one of the fastest growing in the history of the world. The roots of Kwanzaa are in Africa, but the fruits of the tree are truly African-American. Ironically, some of its fruits are reaching back to the motherland from which it sprang as Kwanzaa is celebrated in more and more countries.

Although Kwanzaa is celebrated at the end of the year at the same time as the Christian celebration of Christmas, the Hindu celebration of Divali, the Jewish celebration of Chanukah, and traditional New Year's celebrations, it is not designed as an alternative to or replacement for any of the holidays. Kwanzaa may be celebrated jointly with any or all of the year-end holidays. More importantly, it also offers a time for reflection and self-affirmation, in contrast with the rampant commercialization that has overtaken some of the other holidays.

The celebration of Kwanzaa is guided by the *Nguzo Saba* or Seven Principles. Each day of the week-long festival is devoted to the celebration of one of these building blocks of self-awareness.

Umoja	Unity
Kujichagulia	Self-Determination
Ujima	Collective Work and Responsibility
Ujamaa	Cooperative Economics
Nia	Purpose
Kuumba	Creativity
Imani	Faith

The mystical number seven is at the core of the celebration; there are seven days, seven principles, and even seven symbols of the festival. The symbols are the *mazao,* the fruits and vegetables of the harvest that are a part of the celebration table; the *mkeka,* the placemat on which they are arranged, and the *kinara,* the seven-branched candlestick that holds the red, black, and green candles, the *mishumaa saba,* that are lighted each evening. There are also the *muhindi,* the ears of corn that represent each child still remaining at home; the *kikombe cha umoja,* the communal chalice from which the ceremonial libation is poured; and the *zawadi,* the gifts.

Kwanzaa is essentially a family holiday, whether it be the nuclear family, the extended family, or the communal family. Each evening of the holiday, family members gather around the celebration table to read the Seven Principles and meditate on the principle of the day while the youngest child lights one of the candles. Visitors to the home are asked to participate as the brief nightly ceremony is held, the candles lighted, and libation poured from the communal cup.

There are as many different types of Kwanzaa as there are types of families in the African-American community. African-Ameri-

cans are known for improvisation; our virtuoso turns have created musical forms that have made the entire world sing and
dance. Our artistic endeavors have redefined western art forms.
Wherever we have stepped, our transformational and improvisa-
tional skills have changed the country and the hemisphere in
domains as wide-ranging as retail sales and cooking, music, and
language. In our world, there's always room for improvisation; it
would be impossible for us not to improvise on the themes of
Kwanzaa.

So we ring in changes and create new riffs on our own holiday.
There are single Kwanzaas, celebrated by individuals with
friends and neighbors; nuclear family Kwanzaas with mommy,
daddy, and the kids gathering each evening to light the candles.
There are single-parent Kwanzaas, extended-family Kwanzaas,
neighborhood Kwanzaas, and even community Kwanzaas. Each
celebration brings something else to the kaleidoscope of possibilities that is the holiday.

While the basic *Nguzo Saba* (Seven Principles) remain unchanged,
celebrants are open to find the way to the holiday that best
expresses their individuality. Some followers of Kwanzaa fast
from sunrise to sunset during the seven days, as with the Muslim
Ramadan. Needless to say, this makes the gathering for the
evening meal more celebratory. Others invite different friends in
to celebrate throughout the seven days, or have gatherings to
remind the children of the family of the seven principles. Still others celebrate Kwanzaa without even knowing that they're doing
it. All of those New Year's Eve gatherings and New Year's Day
open houses fall right into the category of the Kwanzaa gatherings, whatever they're called. All that are missing are the *mazao,*
and the *mkeka,* the *kinara* with the *mishumaa saba,* the *muhindi,* the
kikombe cha umoja, and the *zawadi.*

The Kwanzaa that you will find between these pages is my personal Kwanzaa; an individual riff that can be embroidered at
your whim. My aunt Clara always used to say, "You don't have a
holiday, you have to *make* a holiday." In this she spoke the truth.
The personal meaning of each and every holiday comes from the

manner and commitment with which the celebrants choose to participate in it.

My Kwanzaa is informed by two main factors in my life: family and ritual. My family has always been the nucleus of my being. Pride in my parents, their accomplishments, their perseverence, their ability to survive in a world that was not always kind, and a desire to live up to their standards have been strong motivating factors.

I am also an individual steeped in a love of history and tradition. As a teacher, I believe it is important that we know about our past. As an internationalist, I believe it is important that we know about the cultures of peoples of African descent around the globe. As a spiritual being, I believe it is important that we honor those who went before so that we build on their deeds in creating our own future.

I am a newcomer to the holiday of Kwanzaa, but when I look at the holiday, I realize that I've been celebrating it all of my adult life in my own personal way. I've been out of sync, but I've been in the spirit. My personal celebration has taken place on only one of the days of the holiday: January 1. On that day, I open my home to friends old and new, to relatives, and to new acquaintances whose spirits speak to me. Over the eighteen or so years that it's been held, the gathering has grown from a few friends who were invited over to meet my parents to a gathering of fifty or more individuals from around the world.

At last year's celebration, Haitians, Brazilians, Senegalese, Guyanese, Ethiopians, and Americans of all hues gathered to start the year. A Moslem religious leader shared conversation with a Yoruba priestess, while a precocious eleven-year-old offered his views on polygamy to an astonished group of single over-forty women. My eighty-one-year-old mother danced a few vigorous steps to some Zairian *soukouss* music, while my Uncle Herbie, who's really not my uncle but has known me all of my life, guarded the door. There was a heaping plate of food on the floor in the kitchen for my ancestors, who were called by name in a small Yoruba ceremony just prior to the serving of the food. There was music, food, drink, good times, reflection, and communion. In short, there was Kwanzaa.

The menu has always been selected to salute my African-American ancestry and my international life. Each year there's Hoppin' John for luck and collard greens for folding money. There's also roast pork for sheer colored cussedness. A mixture of okra, corn, and tomatoes is served with hot chile to fire us up for the oncoming year and to remind us of our origins. For internationality, there's always a diaspora dish from the Caribbean, or the Motherland, that changes annually.

The gathering has become so much a part of my celebration of the first of the year that my budget and my life are planned around it. Up until recently, there have been none of the more traditional trappings of Kwanzaa, but the spirit of the celebration—the physical and spiritual communion of friends, family, neighbors, and new acquaintances—is exactly what the holiday is about.

As I look around at the African-American community, I find that I have unwittingly allowed myself some leeway because I do not have children. The responsibilities of Kwanzaa, though, extend beyond the family to the extended family and to the community, and there, we all have children. Our children need the sense of specialness that comes from participating in a known and loved ritual. They need the mastery of self-discipline that comes from order. They need the self-awareness that comes from a knowledge of their past. They need Kwanzaa as a tool for building their future and our own.

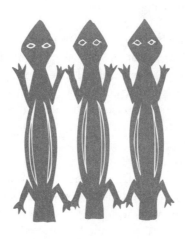

PREPARING FOR KWANZAA

Kwanzaa, whether it's your first or your thirtieth (that's all that are possible), is a joyous time of anticipation and festivity. The holiday takes on greater meaning if as much thought is put into the preparation as goes into the celebration. Begin by reading about the holiday and knowing what its background and purpose are. The best source on that is the work by the man who invented the holiday: Dr. Maulana Karenga. No home that celebrates the holiday should be without a copy of either *Kwanzaa Origin, Concepts, and Practice* (Kawaida, 1975) or *The African-American Holiday of Kwanzaa: A Celebration of Family, Community & Culture* (University of Sankore Press, 1989). Several other works offer personal explanations of the holiday and suggestions for celebrating it. Check with your local bookstore. (This is a good time to practice the principle of *Ujamaa,* cooperative economics; think of the African-American bookstores first.) Think also of local organizations in your town or city that may have communal celebrations of Kwanzaa in which you and your family may wish to participate.

After you have decided just how you wish to celebrate the holiday, be sure that you have the Seven Basic Symbols of Kwanzaa:

• The *mazao,* the fruit and vegetables that represent the roots of the celebration as a harvest ceremony, you can obtain from your greengrocer. (Again, think *Ujamaa.*) Look to those fruits and vegetables emblematic of the African diaspora. Think of pumpkins and squashes, of sweet potatoes and bananas, of watermelons and mangoes, of sugar cane and okra, and of all the bounty of the Motherland and of this hemisphere, bounty that we eat daily. A proverb states, "Before eating, thank the food." In your creation of your Kwanzaa arrangement of *mazao,* think of the fruits and vegetables that have enabled us to survive on both sides of the Atlantic. Cornucopia are inappropriate as they hark back to European traditions. You may, therefore, wish to use African or African-American baskets in organizing your Kwanzaa display. Think of the sweet grass baskets of Senegal, the intricately woven baskets of Kenya, or the incised calabash gourds of Benin. Con-

sider carved wooden bowls from Haiti, red heart trays from Guyana, or Gullah baskets from this side of the Atlantic. As you set up the display, thank the fruits and vegetables for contributing to our survival.

• The *mkeka,* the mat, holds the display together and symbolizes the foundation of the holiday and our foundations as a people. A proverb states, "If you know who you are, you know where you're going." Select a piece of fabric from the African diaspora to serve as your placemat, but not just because it's pretty; know what it is, where it's from, and why you have chosen it. Ghana's *kente* has become a symbol of the Motherland for many of us, but there are other possibilities. Try a piece of Kenya's *kitenge* or Nigeria's *aṣo oke.* A tie-dyed fabric from the Côte d'Ivoire or an austere piece of Malian mudcloth, an intricate piece of Kasai velvet from Zaire, or even a mat hand-crocheted by a family elder could all serve. You may even choose to make your own (see page 67).

• The *kinara,* the candleholder, symbolizes our ancestors and it should be chosen with care, or constructed with love to honor them. In early Kwanzaa celebrations, the *kinara* was used to symbolize *nkulunkulu,* the firstborn, the one who is at the beginning of our people and our principles. First-time celebrants should be reminded that a *kinara* is not a Jewish menorah. The *kinara* has seven branches, each of which holds one of the seven *mishumaa saba.* The candles are placed in the *kinara* with the black candle in the middle, the red candles to the left, and the green candles to the right. Following the first day of Kwanzaa, on which the black central candle is lighted, the candles are lighted alternately from left to right, reinforcing visually the image that without struggle (represented by the red candles), there is no future (represented by the green ones).

• The *muhindi,* the ears of corn, represent the number of children in each household. They signify continuity and potential as corn grows from corn and each ear has the potential within it of becoming a stalk and, in turn, producing other ears. Children represent our continuity and here they are celebrated.

• The *kikombe cha umoja,* the communal cup of unity, symbolizes the unity of all peoples of African descent. It is used to pour *tambiko,* the libation, to the four cardinal points in the honor of the ancestors and also is passed among the celebrants of the holiday as a sign of solidarity. Select a communal cup that speaks culturally to the holiday. It may be a simple gourd or a richly carved wooden chalice.

• The *zawadi,* gifts, are also a part of the holiday celebration. They may be given throughout the holiday or on a particular night to celebrate a special victory with that principle. The *zawadi* of Kwanzaa are not given automatically, but rather given as rewards for promises kept, tasks accomplished, difficulties overcome, and progress made. In selecting Kwanzaa *zawadi,* emphasis should be placed on education and cultural value. Books make excellent gifts, particularily those by African and African-American authors, and those that discuss aspects of our history and culture. Because Kwanzaa aims to avoid the crass commercialization that has overtaken the other year-end festivities, handmade gifts are also particularly appropriate, whether made by the giver or by other African-Americans. Again, as with all Kwanzaa purchases, in purchasing Kwanzaa *zawadi,* the principle of *Ujamaa* should be kept in mind. With Kwanzaa symbols and handmade Kwanzaa gifts, the principle of *Kuumba* should be kept in the forefront.

For all of its serious principles, though, Kwanzaa is also a time of feasting, of rejoicing, of savoring friendships and ties with family, or renewing commitments. Part of that communion of family and friends takes place around the table, and the communion of the table is a good part of the warmth of the holiday. We as a people have for generations communed in the kitchen. We have for generations gathered around scarred wooden tables shelling peas and picking pieces of meat off a chicken or turkey carcass. We've lifted lids off steaming pots of savory stews and slow-cooked vegetables and savored tastes of what's cooking off the edges of wooden spoons. We have come together at thousands of wedding banquets, christening feasts, and family reunions. We have shared sorrows and mourned over funeral meats and casseroles of macaroni and cheese. We have danced with friends, mourned lost loves, advised children, and planned protests around kitchen tables. During the holiday of Kwanzaa, we again come together in our own personal kitchen communion, using the table as a locus for reaffirming our family values, our personhood, and our principles as a people.

The recipes in this book are designed so that all family members, whatever their ages and abilities, can participate in their creation. There are also projects for each night, designed to bring the family together. The projects are simple and can be done by tiny fingers with blunt-edged scissors, or by gnarled hands that are too bent to hold a needle. They are for all the family members. Some work to help the community; some enhance the family and provide a record of growth; some provide continuity and highlight *Kuumba,* creating Kwanzaa symbols for use in future years. There are blank pages throughout the book so that family members can add their own recipes, reminiscences, and history, and create a personal work that will truly be a Kwanzaa keepsake.

Use the book as a building block for your family's Kwanzaa memories, fill it with recipes, photographs, family history, and lore. Write in the margins, fold down the pages at favorite dishes, paste in recipes snipped from other sources. Keep family birthdates and history in between its covers and transform it into a talisman and keepsake for future generations. Kwanzaa is about unity. Never is a family or a group more together than when it sits down to table. During the holiday of Kwanzaa, use the pages of this book and the table-time communion of the holiday to heal old wounds, build new bridges, forge new friendships, and create new futures for your family and for all of our families.

THE GRIOT'S PAGES

 When an old person dies in Africa, it is as though a library had burned.

The Christian Bible says, "In the beginning was the Word." Africans and people of African descent throughout the world understand this only too well. We are a people of the word: juking and jiving, talking and testifying, speechifying and signifying, preaching and teaching. Our *griots* are true masters of the word, savoring each nuance of language and meaning with a delight that is contagious. Think of the sermons of unknown ministers and the songs of the minstrels of Mali. Formerly, our *griots* were unknown bards, troubadours armed with *koras* and harps, drums and cymbals recalling the deeds of heroes like Sundiata of Mali and Chaka of the Zulu. Today, they capture our ephemeral words from the air and place them on paper for the future. Their names are known. They are called Maryse Condé and Maya Angelou, Ismael Reed and Imamu Baraka, Nicolas Guillen and Wole Soyinka, Samuel Selvon and Toni Morrison, Chinua Achebe and "Miss Lou" Bennett, Langston Hughes and Paul Lawrence Dunbar, Zora Neale Hurston, James Baldwin, and more, oh, so many, many more.

Each family has its own *griot* as well, the one who knows the birthdays and the telephone numbers, where the great-aunts are and where great-grandaddy really came from. As this holiday of Kwanzaa will celebrate the ancestors of your family, these pages are where the family *griot* can record your family history. Write the names and birthdays of all of the members of your immediate lineage that you know: mother/father, grandmother/grandfather on each side, and so forth as far back as possible.

FAMILY HISTORY

FAMILY HISTORY

FAMILY HISTORY

FAMILY HISTORY

FAMILY HISTORY

UNITY IN THE FAMILY, COMMUNITY, NATION, AND RACE.

TO STRIVE FOR AND MAINTAIN

THE FIRST NIGHT

UMOJA

UNITY

When spider webs unite they can tie up a lion. —*Ethiopian proverb*

On the first night of the holiday, as on all nights of the holiday, the celebration begins with the asking of the question *Habari gani?* (What's the news?) The answer is the principle of the day. As this is the first day of the holiday, the response is *Umoja.* The lighting of one of the seven candles on the *kinara* and the pouring of libation from the *kikombe cha umoja* follow the asking of the question. On this, the first day of the holiday, the black candle at the center of the *kinara* is lighted. As the candle is lighted, the person lighting the candle should discuss what the principle of *Umoja* means. After the candle is lighted, *tambiko* (libation) is poured to the four cardinal points of the globe. (The pouring of the libation may accompany the saluting of the ancestors with a name called for each of the cardinal points of the compass.) Finally, the communal cup is passed around and the celebrants should sip from it. (If health concerns make sharing a cup inappropriate, then miming a sip is perfectly acceptable.) While *tambiko* is poured, or as the cup is passed, the ancestors are saluted.

Tonight is the night we celebrate the spirit of Umoja (unity).

Tonight and all nights of the year we celebrate the spirits of those who have gone before, who represent the values of Umoja.

We celebrate the spirits of:

Kwame Nkrumah of Ghana
Mae Aninha of Ile Axe Opo Afonja in Brazil
Marcus Garvey of Jamaica
Mary McLeod Bethune of the United States
_____ (your family selection[s])

and the spirits of all others who have gone before who understood the need to maintain unity in families, in our communities, nations, and in our race. We celebrate the spirits of all of those who understood that all children of Mother Africa around the globe share a common heritage and a common destiny.

Tonight and all nights, we celebrate the spirits of all of those who are here with us.

Tonight and all nights, we celebrate the spirits of those who are yet to come.

Following the saluting of the ancestors, there should be a few minutes' conversation about their lives and accomplishments. The brief biographies here are simply springboards to discussion. Each family should add and subtract names from the call as they please in the space provided. In each case, though, all present should know why the spirit has been selected. In this book, I have selected to salute the spirits of those who have gone on to become ancestors. They are selected from the ancestor-spirits of the African-Atlantic world. I have made an effort to select those who are not as well known as some of our other ancestor spirits. I have passed over Malcolm, Martin, and Frederick Douglass in favor of Kwame Nkrumah, Mae Aninha, Marcus Garvey, Mary McLeod Bethune, Fannie Lou Hamer, Nicolas Guillen, and Zumbi in an effort to widen our horizons and push us all beyond the boundaries of our own cultures. When we recognize one another across the divides of language and geography, we are richer for it. These biographies, though, are only the first step. Your family may wish to include those who walk among us and even members of your own family who represent the evening's particular *Nguzo Saba.* Follow the principle of *Kuumba,* creativity, in your own celebration.

KWAME NKRUMAH OF GHANA (1909–1972)

Born in Nkroful in the Western Province of the British Gold Coast (now Ghana), Kwame Nkrumah was the son of a gold-smith. In the traditions of his people, he was named Kwame because he was born on a Saturday. Nkrumah was educated in colonial schools and trained as a teacher at Achimota College. He taught for five years and then journeyed to the United States, where he enrolled at all-Black Lincoln University in Pennsylvania. He attended Lincoln for seven years, receiving Bachelor of Arts and Bachelor of Theology degrees. At the same time he also attended the University of Pennsylvania and received Master of Science and Master of Arts degrees. Nkrumah financed his schooling by working as an unskilled laborer.

Upon completion of his schooling, Nkrumah went to England and became active in anticolonialist Pan-African politics. He was invited to return to Ghana as the secretary of the Gold Coast Convention in 1947. For nine years, Nkrumah fought for the independence of his country. On March 6, 1957, Nkrumah became the prime minister of a state that was renamed Ghana in honor of the ancient African empire. Ghana was the first Black African country to gain its independence from colonial rule. In 1960, a republic was declared and Nkrumah became Ghana's first elected president. Political upheavals followed and Nkrumah was overthrown by a coup in 1966. He died in exile in 1972, yet was buried with full honors at his birthplace. We salute Kwame Nkrumah tonight because he was one of the founding fathers of contemporary Africa.

We salute the spirit of Kwame Nkrumah tonight because as one of the founding fathers of Pan-Africanism, he left us the task of attaining the unity of all peoples of African descent throughout the world.

MAE ANINHA (EUGENIA ANNA DOS SANTOS) OF BRAZIL (1869–1938)

Born July 13, 1869, Eugenia Anna dos Santos lived in a Brazil where slavery was still legal. (It would only be abolished finally in that country in 1888.) The daughter of two Africans of the Grunci nation who had been brought to the city of Salvador da Bahia de Todos os Santos (Bahia), Brazil, she grew up knowing firsthand the poverty and the despair of slavery in the hemisphere. As a youngster, she was initiated into the religion of her ancestors, a religion that celebrated venerated ancestors and the African forces of nature called *orixas* in the Yoruba language spoken in Brazil. She was initiated as a votary of the *orixa* Xango Ogodo and Afonja. Her initiation name in the Yoruba of her ancestors was Oba Biyi, which signaled her devotion to Xango. She studied with her elders and was invited to become a part of the Candomblé of Engenho Velho, better known as Casa Branca. However, following a disagreement over ritual matters, Mae Aninha left the Candomblé and founded her own house.

Later she would purchase land in São Gonçalo do Retiro, then on the outskirts of town, where she would establish her own religious community under the name of Ile Axe Opo Afonja. This community, like Casa Branca from which it sprang and numerous others throughout Brazil, is a living witness to the continuity of African values in the hemisphere. Mae Aninha and others like her throughout the hemisphere maintained their unity with Africa in their praises, saluting the gods of their ancestors and the spirits of their forbears; these New World keepers of Mother Africa's spiritual flames are also links in our chain of unity. Neither politician nor Pan-Africanist, Mae Aninha of Brazil lived the virtues of unity.

We salute the spirit of Eugenia Anna dos Santos (Mae Aninha) tonight as one who was a link in the golden chain that binds us eternally to the continent of our ancestors. We salute her personal vision of the spiritual unity of Africa and the Americas, one that gives us a view to the future while remembering the past.

MARCUS GARVEY OF JAMAICA (1887–1940)

Born at Saint Ann's Bay, Jamaica, on August 17, 1887, Marcus Moziah Garvey spent his youth as an apprentice printer learning firsthand what it meant to be poor and black in colonial Jamaica. Later, while working as a printer, he crystallized the ideas that would lead him, in 1911, to found a small organization with a big name and an even bigger impact: The United Negro Improvement Association (UNIA). The organization was dedicated to the idea that political, military, and economic independence was the only way that the New World's peoples of African origin could uplift themselves. Garvey called for self-reliance for Africans, "at home and abroad."

By 1916, Jamaica had become too small a forum for his then radical ideas, and Garvey, after traveling in Central and South America, settled in New York's Harlem, where he founded another branch of the UNIA. He began to speak of a "Back to Africa" movement. The UNIA grew in size as discussion of repatriation to Africa became a watchword for many African-Americans. With contributions from interested people, Garvey established a newspaper, *Negro World,* opened branches of the UNIA throughout the country, and even formed the Black Star Line, a steamship company designed to transport descendants back to Africa. It was not to be. Garvey's negotiations with the state of Liberia fell through and legal and financial difficulties ensued, resulting in Garvey's being jailed for mail fraud in 1925. He was deported to Jamaica in 1927 and died in London in 1940.

We salute the spirit of Marcus Moziah Garvey tonight because he dared to dream self-reliance and the unity of all Africans at home and abroad. We salute him because he took steps to fulfill that dream and because he left us his dream to attain.

MARY M(LEOD BETHUNE (1875–1955)

Born near the cotton fields of Mayesville, South Carolina, to former slaves, Mary Mcleod Bethune was one of seventeen children. Her parents instilled in her a lifelong love for education by selecting her as the only one of their children to be sent to school. It was felt that she would, in turn, teach her sisters and brothers. She attended local schools and then Scotia College in North Carolina and Moody Bible Institute in Chicago. She honored her promise and taught her siblings. She so took to teaching that, as a young woman, she moved to Daytona, Florida, and founded her own school for African-American women with $1.50 in cash, five students, and a rented cottage. She drilled her students in basic academics and religion and insisted on giving them skills that would enable them to find work once thay left. By 1923 the school numbered a student body of 300 and had a staff of twenty-five. It would ultimately become Bethune-Cookman College.

Mary McLeod Bethune was an active clubwoman with a particular interest in giving African-American women a voice. To that end, she founded the National Council of Negro Women in 1935 and served as the organization's president until 1949. An adviser to presidents, Bethune directed the Division of Negro Affairs of the National Youth Administration during Franklin Delano Roosevelt's New Deal. As the first African-American woman to head a federal office, she was a force in F.D.R.'s Washington, working to remind leaders of the African-American political presence.

We salute the spirit of Mary McLeod Bethune tonight because she taught us the virtues of dreaming and of making those dreams become reality. We salute her tonight, for although she had much, she reached back in her family and beyond her family to her community and her race to bring people together under the banner of unity. We salute her tonight because she said, "Look at me. I am black. I am beautiful."

The menu celebrating UMOJA is a multinational supper celebrating the union of all peoples of African descent throughout the world, from Texas to Tunis, Savannah to Salvador da Bahia, and New York to Nigeria.

Appetizers
SEASONED OLIVES
PAN-ROASTED ALMONDS

Salad
FRESH GREENS WITH AVOCADO AND RASPBERRIES
LIGHT SOY/SESAME DRESSING

Main Dish
MECHOUI-STYLE LEG OF LAMB WITH CUMIN, MINT, AND CHILE

Condiment
MINT NECTARINE CHUTNEY

Starch
ORZO WITH SLIVERED ALMONDS

Dessert
PLAIN CAKE WITH DRAMBUIE APRICOT SAUCE

Beverage
CLASSIC RUM PUNCH

SEASONED OLIVES

SERVES 6 TO 8

In Brazil, olives frequently appear on the table as appetizers to heighten the appetite before a meal. This is probably a part of the nation's Lusitanian heritage.

In North America, the olives are frequently the canned variety. They are given additional flavor and zest by adding herbs and spices to them and allowing them to take on new flavors. This is one variation; you can use your own favorite seasonings to create a variety that is all your own.

1 pound canned ripe olives, drained
1 tablespoon dried thyme
1 teaspoon minced garlic
1 teaspoon minced fresh habanero
  or other hot chile, to taste

2 tablespoons extra-virgin olive oil
Salt and freshly ground black pepper,
  to taste

 Drain the olives and prick each one several times with the point of a sharp knife or a fork.

Place all of the ingredients in a medium-sized bowl and mix them together well with a wooden spoon, making sure that all of the seasonings are well distributed. Cover with plastic wrap and refrigerate overnight. Serve chilled.

The olives will keep for a week or so in the refrigerator, if they last that long.

PAN-ROASTED ALMONDS

•••••••••••
SERVES 6

Driving into the Ourika Valley outside of Marrakesh, Morocco, one may be stopped along the way by small boys selling geodes. When these dull rocks are broken open, they reveal crystalline forms of amethyst and other brilliant delights. The same young boys also sell almonds, wonderful almonds that have a taste like those nowhere else on earth. The same almonds can be purchased, raw, roasted, or sugar-toasted, at the vendors' stalls in Marrakesh's Djema el Fna, the legendary square where jugglers and itinerant dentists, merchants, and magicians meet.

Almonds frequently turn up in the cooking of Morocco. Here, though, they're just blanched and then pan-roasted to a golden brown for a before-dinner nibble.

2 cups shelled almonds   Salt to taste (optional)
2 tablespoons virgin olive oil

Place 4 cups of water in a medium-sized saucepan and bring to a boil. Plunge the almonds into the boiling water and allow them to boil for 2 minutes.

Drain the almonds and, when slightly cooled, slip the brown skins from the almond kernels with your hands. Discard the skins and reserve the kernels.

Heat 1 tablespoon of the olive oil in a heavy cast-iron skillet. Add half of the almonds to the skillet and toast them in the oil, stirring occasionally, until they are golden brown. Drain them on paper towels. Repeat the process with the remaining olive oil and the other half of the almonds. Salt the almonds to taste, if desired, by placing them in a plastic bag with some salt and shaking them until they are evenly coated. Serve warm.

The almonds will keep for a few weeks in the refrigerator, but they are better when prepared fresh, so make small batches.

FRESH GREENS WITH AVOCADO AND RASPBERRIES

•••••••••••••••••••

SERVES 6 TO 8

Many people of African descent are meat- and potato-eaters, preferring to get their vegetables in slow-cooked stews and soups. With today's concerns about healthy eating, though, salads are coming to the fore and we're using ingredients from around the world in testimony to the increasing internationality of the African diaspora.

This salad is a simple one of light fresh greens, tropical avocados, and the sweet surprise of forced winter raspberries. It's dressed with a light dressing prepared with a hint of sesame oil.

3 medium-sized heads Boston lettuce	1 small sweet onion
2 ripe Hass avocados	½ cup fresh raspberries
	Light Soy / Sesame Dressing (page 40)

Wash and clean the lettuce. Discard the tough outside leaves, pick over each leaf to remove brown spots and dirt, and tear the lettuce leaves into bite-sized pieces. Pat the leaves dry on paper towels and place them in a large glass salad bowl.

Peel and pit the avocados, cut them into 1-inch dice, and add them to the salad bowl.

Peel the onion and cut it crosswise into very thin slices. Separate the slices into rings and add them to the salad bowl as well.

Finally, wash the raspberries, picking over them to remove any spoiled ones, and add them to the salad bowl. Pour the dressing over the salad, toss, and serve immediately.

LIGHT SOY/SESAME DRESSING

• • • • • • • • • • • • • • • •

⅓ cup light low-sodium soy sauce
⅓ cup light rice wine vinegar
1 tablespoon sesame oil
2 tablespoons water

¼ teaspoon brown sugar, or to taste
Salt and freshly ground black pepper,
   to taste

Place all of the ingredients together in a small bowl and whisk them until they are well mixed. (The sugar is to cut the tartness of the vinegar, and you may find that you want a bit more or less depending on the type of rice wine vinegar you use.) When the ingredients are well mixed, drizzle the dressing over the salad and serve.

MECHOUI-STYLE LEG OF LAMB WITH CUMIN, MINT, AND CHILE

• • • • • • • • • • • • • • • •

SERVES 6 TO 8

In Senegal, West Africa, in a small restaurant in Les Almadies called CHEZ M'BAYE M'BARRIK, I first tasted the dish called MECHOUI. This festive dish of spit-roasted lamb is traditional in much of the Magreb and has made its way down to Senegal. At the restaurant, diners are presented with a whole roasted baby lamb and they pick off succulent bits to eat with their fingers. I've had variations of this wonderful dish in Senegal, in Tunisia, and in Morocco. In each place, the dish is slightly differently seasoned, as the tastes of the region and indeed of the country influence the taste of the MECHOUI.

This is a variation on the MECHOUI theme that I've come up with. It uses a leg of lamb and a dry marinade combining the North African tastes of mint and cumin with the sub-Saharan African taste of chile. Leftovers can be used to make a quick dish of curried lamb.

1 (4- to 5-pound) shank end half leg
  of lamb
3 cloves garlic, slivered
2 tablespoons virgin olive oil
1 tablespoon salt
1 tablespoon freshly ground black
  pepper

1 tablespoon powdered cumin
2 tablespoons dried mint
⅛ teaspoon powdered habanero
  chile or other hot chile powder, or
  to taste

Preheat the oven to 450 degrees. Trim all excess fat and the fell from the lamb, then pierce the lamb skin with 15 or so small incisions. Insert the garlic slivers into the slits. Slather the olive oil over the lamb and rub it in with your hands. Place the salt, black pepper, cumin, mint, and chile in a spice grinder and pulse until they are well mixed. Then pat them over the lamb, covering the entire leg well. Place the lamb on a rack in a roasting pan.

Place the lamb in the oven and allow it to roast at 450 degrees for 15 minutes. Then lower the heat to 350 degrees and continue to roast the lamb for an additional hour, or until the internal temperature registers 140 degrees for rare, 150 degrees for medium, or 160 degrees for well done on a meat thermometer. (Cooking times will vary according to the shape of the lamb and the heat of your oven.)

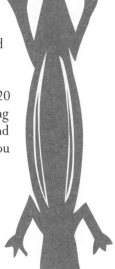

Allow the meat to rest at room temperature for 20 minutes, then carve and serve. You'll be eating your *mechoui*-style leg of lamb with a knife and fork, but it will be tastier and more tender if you carve it parallel to the bone in long thin slices.

MINT NECTARINE CHUTNEY

MAKES ABOUT 2 CUPS

When I was a child, roast lamb was never served without the accompanying mint jelly. The combination of the coolness of the mint and the taste of the lamb was just perfect.

Today the habit of eating spicy condiments with roasted meats is growing in the African-Atlantic world. The mint jelly of my childhood has given way to numerous condiments, some hot, some fiery, some spicy. This chutney is one that I have been playing around with since 1985, when I wrote a book about peppers and chiles around the world called HOT STUFF. In this version the freshness of the mint is highlighted with the taste of nectarines and given a bit of kick with hot chile.

1 bunch fresh mint leaves (approximately ten 3-inch-long sprigs)
3 large, firm nectarines, peeled, pitted, and coarsely chopped
¼ teaspoon minced fresh habanero or other hot chile, or to taste
1 piece fresh ginger (1 inch), scraped
2 cloves garlic
1 small onion, coarsely chopped
½ cup cider vinegar
½ cup sugar

Wash the mint, pull the leaves from the tough stems, and place the leaves in the bowl of a food processor, discarding stems. Add the nectarines, chile, ginger, garlic, and onion and pulse until you have a thick paste. (You may have to drizzle in a bit of the vinegar to get the mixture going.) Continue to pulse until all of the ingredients are pulverized.

Place the paste in a medium-sized nonreactive saucepan and add the remaining vinegar and the sugar, stirring them in well to make sure that they are evenly mixed. Place the saucepan on the heat and bring it slowly to a boil. Reduce the heat and simmer, stirring occasionally, for 30 minutes, or until the chutney has thickened and taken on a jamlike consistency. Be careful not to let the bottom of the chutney burn or stick to the saucepan during the final minutes of cooking.

When the chutney is ready, spoon it into scalded glass jars, allow it to cool, and refrigerate it until it is to be served. The chutney is particularly good with lamb, but will go well with any roasted or grilled meat. It will keep in the refrigerator for 2 to 3 days.

ORZO WITH SLIVERED ALMONDS

····················

SERVES 6 TO 8

Cooking rice is a fine art. While it would seem simple to many, it is all too easy to transform the delicate dish into a coagulated glob of white paste. With this in mind, I sometimes cheat by using orzo, the rice-shaped pasta, for white rice. In this case, I jazz up the orzo with the addition of some slivers of almonds and a dash of orange-flower water. (You can keep a few pan-roasted almonds back from the hungry hordes after you've prepared the appetizer.)

5 quarts water
1 tablespoon virgin olive oil
1 (1-pound) box orzo
¼ cup Pan-Roasted Almonds
  (page 38), slivered

½ teaspoon orange-flower water
  (optional)
Orange segments, for garnish
Chopped parsley, for garnish

Bring the water and olive oil to a boil in a large saucepan. Add the orzo and cook for 7 minutes. Then add the slivered almonds and continue to cook for 3 minutes, or until the orzo is completely cooked. Drain the orzo and, if you choose, sprinkle it with the orange-flower water. Serve hot, garnished with orange segments and parsley.

DRAMBUIE APRICOT SAUCE

MAKES ABOUT 2 CUPS

I am not a dessert eater by nature. In fact, it was only a few years ago that I noticed that visitors to my home were not terribly happy when at the end of the meal I happily presented them with a good cup of coffee and a fresh fruit salad. I've learned my lesson and have been truly humbled.

The African-American way with sweets is serious, and folks want dessert! I'm still not a dessert fan, but I've learned a whole bagful of tricks that will produce a dessert to make any sugar freak smile with delight. This thick apricot-based sauce redolent of Drambuie is one of them. It's excellent when served with a plain yellow cake. You can make your cake from scratch or from a doctored-up mix, or you can buy one from the local bakery.

1 cup dried apricots
2 tablespoons apricot nectar
1 teaspoon fresh lemon juice

⅔ cup apricot preserves
2 tablespoons Drambuie liqueur, or to taste

Place the dried apricots in a saucepan, add water to cover, and bring to a boil over high heat. Then lower the heat and allow the apricots to simmer for 10 minutes, or until they are plumped. Drain the apricots and snip them into small pieces with kitchen shears, and set them aside.

Place the apricot nectar, lemon juice, apricot preserves, and Drambuie in the bowl of a food processor and pulse until you have a thick syrup.

Remove the syrup to a bowl, add the snipped apricots, and stir them in so that each piece is well coated with the liquid.

The sauce can be refrigerated for half an hour and served chilled, or it can be placed in a saucepan and warmed. Either way, it transforms plain cake into something special.

CLASSIC RUM PUNCH

Rum is the classical beverage of the Caribbean. No self-respecting Guyanese, Haitian, Jamaican, or Trinidadian party would ever think of beginning without at least one bottle of rum on the table. Rum is a part of those of us who were brought to those shores; they were brought to work the cane and the cane produced the rum. It is only fitting that on the first night of Kwanzaa, those who partake of alcohol celebrate unity with those from the Caribbean region with a glass of rum.

In much of the Caribbean area, the first rum out of the bottle is traditionally poured on the ground for the ancestors. A Caribbean friend of mine tells tales of how her mother despaired of ever having a living room rug because her father insisted that the area around his chair be free from encumbrances so that he could pour his rum onto the floor. You may use the first pouring of your bottle tonight in the KIKOMBE CHA UMOJA to salute the spirits of all of those who went before, whether from the Caribbean region or not. With the rest, why not prepare a classic rum punch? The popular saying goes:

ONE OF SOUR
TWO OF SWEET
THREE OF STRONG
FOUR OF WEAK

The sour is freshly squeezed lime juice. The sweet is sugar or sugar syrup. The strong is the rum. (Purchase the best you can afford; yes, there is a difference!) The weak is water to round it off. Whether for a single drink or a vat, the one, two, three, four system will keep you on the right track. Drink moderately: it goes down easy but it packs a true kick!

PROJECT

One of the aims of Kwanzaa is to bring together families and friends in productive ways. To this end, each night will conclude with a project. The project can be done on the night or it can be done at any time during the holiday or the year to culminate in a Kwanzaa gift for the following year.

On the first night of Kwanzaa *Umoja,* family unity, is saluted with the creation of a cookbook of family favorites. Most of us know only too well that we never ask for the recipe for something until it is too late. When grandma's gone, we wish we knew how to make her beaten biscuits. When Aunt Dorcas moves away, we wish we had watched exactly how she fluted the edges of her pies.

Begin this first night of Kwanzaa by making a conscious effort to write down the favorite recipes of your family. Have each family member select a favorite recipe to work on. Start by using the blank pages in this book. Then, collect the recipes on sheets of paper to be kept in a file folder or a blank book. Add to the collection throughout the year as holidays and birthdays and special family times bring new recipes to mind. At the end of the year, make copies and present them to other family members: a child going away to college, those leaving for another town. Keep the project growing and developing. It will help to keep the family together and it will preserve your traditions for another generation.

FAMILY RECIPES

FAMILY RECIPES

SPEAK FOR OURSELVES INSTEAD OF BEING DEFINED, NAMED, CREATED FOR, AND SPOKEN FOR BY OTHERS.

TO DEFINE OURSELVES, NAME OURSELVES, CREATE FOR OURSELVES,

THE SECOND NIGHT

KUJICHAGULIA

SELF-DETERMINATION

Nobody will think you're somebody if you don't think so yourself.
—Traditional African-American expression

On the second night of the holiday, as on all nights of the holiday, the celebration begins with the pouring of libation from the *kikombe cha umoja* and the lighting of one of the seven candles of the *kinara*. Tonight the central black candle of *Umoja* and the first of the red candles on the left of the *kinara*, the candle of *Kujichagulia*, self-determination, are lighted. After the candles are lighted, libation is poured or the *kikombe cha umoja* is passed around and thoughts turn to the spirits of those who represented the virtues of *Kujichagulia* in our society.

Tonight is the night we celebrate the spirit of Kujichagulia (self-determination).

Tonight and all nights of the year, we celebrate the spirits of those who have gone before who represent the values of Kujichagulia.

We celebrate the spirits of:

Chaka Zulu of South Africa
Zumbi of Palmares in Brazil
Nanny of the Maroons in Jamaica
Cinque of the Amistad in the United States
_____ (your family selection[s])

and the spirits of all others who fought and died defining themselves, determining their destinies, and forging their futures and our own.

Tonight and all nights, we celebrate the spirits of all those who are here with us.

Tonight and all other nights, we celebrate the spirits of those who are yet to come.

CHAKA ZULU OF SOUTH AFRICA

Born the son of Nandi and Sanza'ngakona, in southern Africa in the first half of the nineteenth century, Chaka was a solitary child. His father was a leader of one of the clans of the Abatetwa, but because questions were raised about his legitimacy, Chaka spent much of his childhood treated as illegitimate and as an outcast. These hardships, though, only served to nurture the man that Chaka would become. He grew into a man of impressive physical strength and soon became a *mampoli,* or chieftain, to whom remarkable deeds were attributed. His actions only increased the jealousy of his half brothers.

His life threatened, Chaka found refuge with his father's sovereign, Dinguiswayo, and became his trusted adviser and spokesman. He rapidly rose in the ranks, and on the death of his father recouped his rightful inheritance and became chief of his clan. His military valor became known, and in the political instability that followed the defeat and death of Dinguiswayo, he became the head of the majority of the Ngouni people. He celebrated his sovereignty by changing their name to one that sounded like the drums of wars or the thunders of the heavens: *Zulu* (which means sky) or *Amazulus* (meaning people from the sky). He cemented his reign by reorganizing the armies into a military machine where training, strategy, and discipline were the watchwords. The army was divided into regiments of about a thousand individuals of about the same age. No detail was too small for Chaka's scrutiny. Sandals were eliminated because they slowed the warriors down; the throwing lance was eliminated in favor of the *assegai,* the spear or javelin, which encouraged close offensive hand-to-hand combat.

Chaka and his armies, with their new military might and their formidable strategy, overran southern Africa like a juggernaut. Chaka was a military man and constant war was the order of his empire. The circumstances surrounding his death are unknown, but it seems likely that he was assassinated in a political plot instigated by his half brothers. His legendary final words reminded his murderers that they would not rule for long, for the whites were coming to drive them out. His descendants and other black South Africans have only recently returned to power in the land that was once theirs, thanks to the victories of Chaka Zulu.

We salute Chaka tonight as a man who has made his mark on history, one who united a dispersed people and moved them on to glory. We salute his skill as determining his own destiny and that of his people.

ZUMBI OF PALMARES IN BRAZIL

Born within the precincts of the Northeastern Brazilian state of Pernambuco in 1655, Zumbi was unlike other blacks born in Brazil in that period, who were automatically doomed to lives of enslavement. He was different; he was special; he was free! Zumbi was free because he was born within the stockaded walls of the legendary but oh, so real *quilombo* or Maroon settlement of former slaves, known as Palmares. Palmares, a name that still resonates today, was a settlement established by runaway slaves; it grew to a community of several thousand people and lasted in the mountains of Pernambuco for more than fifty years.

Zumbi was born in Palmares, but as a baby, he was captured in one of the periodic raids on the *quilombo*. He was given as a present to a priest in Porto Calvo who raised him and named him Francisco. The priest educated the small black boy, teaching him Latin, Portuguese, and Catholicism, but he could not rid him of the taste of freedom on his tongue.

In 1670, Francisco ran away and returned to the mountains and the Palmares of his birth. The Palmares to which he returned was a loosely knit confederation of villages covering six thousand square kilometers; all under the rule of Ganga Zumba. At its height in 1672, Ganga Zumba's reign slipped into decline by 1680, when Zumbi assumed the mantle of leadership and prepared for war. He fortified parts of Palmares, surrounding strategic areas with stockades and palisades, and prepared to fight off the constant attacks from the sugar lords of Pernambuco whose slaves looked to Palmares as salvation. The battles lasted for more than ten years, but finally, in January 1694, the final fight for Palmares began with a series of engagements equaled in size only by the Brazilian War of Independence 130 years later. The main part of Palmares fell on the sixth of February. For years, it was thought that Zumbi had died in a dramatic leap to his death off the edge of the abyss that made Palmares such a formidable fortress, but recent evidence suggests that he survived, along with about two thousand others, and continued to wage a guerrilla war against the colonial forces until November 1695, when he was betrayed and killed, leaving behind him the history of Palmares and a legacy of resistance to the domination of others.

We salute Zumbi of Palmares tonight because, born free, he worked, fought, and died to maintain that freedom and to ensure the freedom and self-determination of others.

NANNY OF THE MAROONS IN JAMAICA

Where and when Nanny was born is lost in the whispering winds of history, but her importance to the people of Jamaica is written in tablets of stone. Whether she was born in Jamaica or in Africa is as unknown as the actual date of her birth, but it is thought that Nanny was the sister of Cudjoe, a renowned Jamaican rebel leader of the Maroons, who had their origins as escaped Spanish slaves, and that she never personally experienced slavery. It is also thought that she had no children of her own, but all of the people of her community became her children; she was the mother of her people in the traditional sense of the Ashanti Queen Mothers.

The community Nanny led was known as the Windward Maroons and had its capital at Nanny Town. It was thought to have been founded in the 1690s and consisted of over 600 acres in the Back Rio Grande Valley in Portland, Jamaica. Much of the land was located on the northern slopes of the Blue Mountains. This community was ruled by Nanny when the town was found by the English in the 1730s. The English, after "discovering" the community, attempted to capture the town. Fierce fighting between the English and Maroons broke out and continued throughout the years of the First Maroon Wars. Nanny dominated the Maroon fighting, not by actively participating herself, but rather by blessing the guerrilla fighters and directing the campaign strategy. Maroons fought by ambush, using stealth and their knowledge of the terrain to defeat their enemies. Nanny communicated with her forces via the Maroon *abeng,* a bugle carved from a cow horn, that could be heard throughout the mountain valleys and could be played so adeptly that the warriors could be summoned as though they were spoken to.

A priestess to her people, Nanny had powers beyond those of mere mortals: She was said to be able to catch bullets in her buttocks, rendering them harmless, and then return them; this power was called *nantucompong* in the Akan language that the Maroons retained from their African past. Foremost among the resistance leaders of her time, Nanny was determined never to cede to the English and made a trans-island trek with her people to avoid surrendering. She continued fighting until she reluctantly accepted peace terms in 1738. An unvanquished leader, she was granted a land parcel in Portland by truce agreement in 1740 and continued to rule in peace until she died in the 1750s. She rests in Jamaican soil, a hero of the Jamaican nation, ever free and ever faithful to her ideals.

We salute Nanny of the Maroons tonight for her fierce, unswerving determination to guard the liberty of her people and to ensure that they and only they determined who they were.

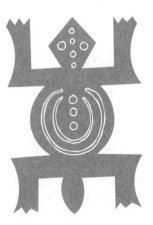

CINQUE OF THE <u>AMISTAD</u> IN THE UNITED STATES

No one is sure when the horrible journey began, but its second phase started in June of 1839 when forty-nine men and four children newly arrived from the African coast were herded into the hold of a slave ship ironically called the *Amistad* (Friendship), lying at anchor off the coast of Havana, Cuba. Many of the ship's captives were of the Mende people of Sierra Leone, among them Cinque, a twenty-five-year-old rice farmer and son of Mende nobles. The ship laden with captives for resale was bound for another part of Cuba, but it was not destined to arrive. The combination of a lax crew and a remarkably efficient group of Africans under the direction of Cinque resulted in one of history's most successful shipboard slave insurrections.

Overpowering the captain and cook, the men took control of the ship and ordered the Spaniards to sail them back to the West African coast, toward the rising sun. The Spaniards did so, but only by day, setting course by night for the northwest, where after a journey of two months they came into waters off the coast of Long Island. Cinque ordered anchor to be dropped and went ashore to attempt to secure provisions, but before the ship could set sail again, it was seized by an American naval vessel and taken to Connecticut. As mutineers, the captives were in danger of being extradited to Cuba to stand trial, a course favored by the Cuban and Spanish governments and then-president Van Buren, who wished to avoid a diplomatic incident. However, Spain had outlawed slave importation into its territories, including Cuba, in 1817, and so the captives were not legally slaves. The matter was to be determined by the American judicial system in a trial that lasted eighteen months, going all the way to the Supreme Court, where former president John Quincy Adams pleaded the captives' cause, winning the day. It was agreed that they had been illegally sold and were not slaves. They were free. However, there were no funds for repatriation. Abolitionists eventually raised the money to send the Africans home and thirty-five survivors of the original fifty-three returned to Africa, narrowly escaping the voracious jaws of New World slavery.

Tonight, we salute the spirit of Cinque and the spirits of all his fellow captives of the *Amistad*. Despite overwhelming odds, they fought to determine their destinies and succeeded. They lost their freedom, dreamed of recapturing it, fought for freedom, and attained it. Their faith and their attainments are beacons to us all.

The meal celebrating the NGUZO SABA of KUJICHAGULIA is an "Out of Africa" menu comprised of a variety of dishes from the Motherland that celebrate our African roots.

Appetizer

SOUTH AFRICAN SWEET POTATO FRITTERS

Salad

MOROCCAN-STYLE GRILLED PEPPER SALAD

Main Dish

SENEGALESE CHICKEN YASSA

Starch

PLAIN WHITE RICE

Condiment

PIMENT AIMÉE

(AIMÉE'S HOT SAUCE)

Dessert

CARAMELIZED RIPE PLANTAINS

Beverage

THE NAA NAA MAROCAIN

(MOROCCAN MINT TEA)

SOUTH AFRICAN SWEET POTATO FRITTERS

SERVES 6 TO 8

Throughout the African continent, frying in deep oil is a culinary art form. The making of fritters and snacks by frying tasty tidbits in various oils has crossed the Atlantic with Africa's children to become emblematic of African cooking in the Western Hemisphere as well. Dishes like New Orleans rice fritters or CALAS; *the Caribbean's codfish fritters, whether they're called* BACALAITOS *or* ACRAS DE MORUE; *and Brazil's ambrosial* ACARAJE *all hark back to this tradition.*

The sweet potato fritters that begin this night's menu are a South African invention. They, like variations of this dish throughout the continent, combine the sweet potato, a New World tuber, with an African culinary technique. One of the tricks to great fritters is to use clean oil and to make sure that the oil is hot enough before beginning.

These fritters can be accompanied by a spicy hot sauce when served as an appetizer course. Alternatively, they can be lightly dusted with sugar and served as a dessert.

Peanut oil for frying
  1 pound sweet potatoes, peeled
  ½ cup flour

1 egg, beaten
Salt and freshly ground black pepper,
  to taste

 Heat 2 inches of oil in a heavy saucepan or fryer to 375 degrees.

Grate the sweet potatoes into medium-sized bowl, cover them with boiling water, and let them stand for 15 minutes. Drain off the water and slowly add the remaining ingredients, stirring to make sure that they are well mixed. You should have a thickish paste that will hold its shape when picked up in a tablespoon. If the mixture is too thick, add a bit of warm water. If it is too thin, add a bit more flour.

Drop the mixture, a few tablespoons at a time, into the hot oil and cook the fritters for 3 to 5 minutes, or until they float to the surface, turning them once to make sure that they are slightly browned on each side. Drain on absorbent paper and serve hot.

MOROCCAN-STYLE GRILLED PEPPER SALAD

SERVES 6 TO 8

Formal meals in Morocco are lengthy events. The guests, who are seated on banquettes around low circular tables, are regaled with the best the household has to offer. Frequently the first course is a selection of small plates of vegetable salads, which are eaten with crusty pieces of flat bread. This salad is a variation on the traditional Moroccan salad known as SLATA FELFEL. (FELFEL means pepper in Arabic.)

If you want to make this dish even more special for Kwanzaa, you can use red, green, and the deep eggplant-hued bell peppers that are almost black for a black, red, and green salad.

1 pound mixed red and green bell peppers
3 tablespoons extra-virgin olive oil
1 tablespoon fresh lemon juice
½ teaspoon ground cumin
¼ teaspoon finely minced fresh cilantro (leaf coriander)

2 teaspoons finely chopped flat-leaf parsley
Salt and freshly ground black pepper, to taste

Place the peppers on a rack under the broiler and grill them until they are charred black on the outside, turning them frequently. When they are charred, wrap them in paper towels and let them stand for 10 minutes or more; this will make the skin come off more easily. With a sharp paring knife, peel and core the bell peppers, cut them into long thin strips, and arrange them on a serving dish.

Whisk the olive oil, lemon juice, cumin, cilantro, parsley, salt, and pepper together in a small bowl and drizzle over the pepper strips. Serve warm or at room temperature.

SENEGALESE CHICKEN YASSA

••••••••••••
SERVES 6

This has become my good luck dish. It was one of the first African dishes that I tasted and it was truly love at first bite. I so love this traditional dish from the Casamance region of southern Senegal that I've demonstrated making it on television and taught it to many folk in cooking classes around the country.

This variation on the classic YASSA theme uses carrots and pimiento-stuffed olives to create a rich chicken stew.

I often double this recipe because yassa is even better the next day. It also freezes well.

¼ cup fresh lemon juice
4 large onions, thinly sliced
Salt and freshly ground black pepper, to taste
⅛ teaspoon minced fresh habanero or other hot chile, to taste
¼ cup plus 1 tablespoon peanut oil
One chicken (2½ to 3½ pounds), cut into serving pieces

1 habanero or other hot chile, pricked with a fork
½ cup pimiento-stuffed olives
4 carrots, scraped and thinly sliced
1 tablespoon Dijon-style mustard
½ cup water

In a large nonreactive bowl, prepare a marinade with the lemon juice, onions, salt, pepper, minced chile, and the ¼ cup peanut oil. Place the chicken pieces in the marinade, making sure that they are all well covered, and allow them to marinate for at least 2 hours in the refrigerator.

Preheat the broiler. Remove the chicken pieces, reserving the marinade, and place them in a shallow roasting pan. Broil them until they are lightly browned on both sides. Remove the onions from the marinade. Cook them slowly in the remaining 1 tablespoon oil in a flameproof 3-quart casserole or dutch oven until tender and transluscent. Add the remaining marinade and heat through.

When the liquid is thoroughly heated, add the broiled chicken pieces, the pricked chile, the olives, carrots, mustard, and water. Stir to mix well, then bring the yassa slowly to a boil. Lower the heat and simmer for about 20 minutes, or until the chicken is cooked through. Serve hot over white rice.

PLAIN WHITE RICE

SERVES 6 TO 8

The real staff of life to many African-Americans, even more than wheat- or corn-based products, rice is a part of our heritage. Many of our ancestors who lived in the area of West Africa known as the grain coast were involved in the cultivation of an African variant of rice long before Europeans arrived on the continent. Their knowledge was forcibly transported to the Carolinas, where it was used as the backbone of the Carolina rice industry. Rice is also grown in other parts of the hemisphere; it is astonishing to drive along roads in countries like Haiti and suddenly find rice paddies.

Rice turns up in our meals in all forms from appetizer fritters to dessert puddings, and is eaten at any time of the day, from breakfast to midnight snack. There are many ways to prepare white rice; this is the simplest.

3⅓ cups water
1⅓ cups uncooked rice

1 teaspoon salt
1 tablespoon butter

Bring the water to a boil in a medium-sized saucepan. Stir in the rice, salt, and butter. Cover, lower the heat, and simmer for about 20 minutes, or until the rice is fork-tender. Remove the rice pot from the heat and allow it to stand, covered, for 5 minutes, until all of the water has been absorbed.

Fluff the rice into a serving bowl with a fork and serve hot with additional butter or gravy.

PIMENT AIMÉE
(AIMÉE'S HOT SAUCE)

MAKES ABOUT ½ CUP

My friend Aimée is one of the best West African cooks I know. Born in Niger to a Dahomean father and a Nigerian mother, she has traveled the world, living in Paris and various countries of West Africa before finding her current roost in Dakar. Aimée's food reflects the influences of all the places she has lived, while maintaining a firm grounding in the West African states that are her home. Whatever she serves, whether it's an oh-so-French steak frites or a poulet yassa, she always has a small dish of her homemade chile condiment on the table.

When Aimée comes to visit me in the States, we head first to my greengrocer. There we stock up on habanero chiles so that she can make a small jar of her special PIMENT, which she then packs and takes with her to her other destinations.

10 habanero or other hot chiles
3 cloves garlic

1 small onion, roughly chopped
½ teaspoon salt, to taste

Place the chiles, garlic, onion, and salt in the bowl of a food processor or blender and pulse until they are a grainy paste. Spoon the paste into a scalded small jar and cover tightly. The paste will keep for several weeks in the refrigerator and should be used very sparingly as an on-table condiment, or to add extra zing to virtually any dish.

CARAMELIZED RIPE PLANTAINS

SERVES 6 TO 8

Plantains turn up everywhere in West African cooking. They're nibbled as street snacks, pounded into mashes and FOOFOOS, added to soups and stews, and served as dessert.

Plantains are used at virtually every stage of their maturing process. The green ones are peeled, sliced, and deep-fried as chips. The ripe yellow ones are used as a starch to accompany main dishes, and the superripe black ones in which the starch has turned to sugar appear as desserts. This is one way to serve plantain that appeals to everyone.

4 ripe plantains
1 tablespoon butter

1 tablespoon sugar

Peel the plantains and slice them into ½-inch rounds. Heat the butter to foaming in a heavy skillet over medium heat. Add the plantain slices to the butter and cook for 5 to 8 minutes, or until they are lightly browned and slightly caramelized. Sprinkle the plantain slices with the sugar, allow the sugar to caramelize slightly, then remove the plantains from the skillet. Serve warm.

These plantain slices are also particularly good when served over vanilla ice cream, topped with the caramelized butter from the pan.

THE <u>NAA NAA MAROCAIN</u> (MOROCCAN MINT TEA)

•••••••••••••••••••
SERVES 6 TO 8

Mint tea is served in Morocco and in Senegal. Prepared with much ceremony, it traditionally uses loaf sugar and fresh mint for a taste that is unforgettable and somewhat habit-forming.

This mint tea is a simple one, using lump sugar; it has a teaspoon of dried verbena added to the fresh mint for a different taste. Traditionally, mint tea is served in small glasses that are held with the tips of one's fingers.

4 teaspoons Chinese green tea
1 bunch (6 to 8 sprigs) fresh
   peppermint

1 tablespoon dried verbena*
Sugar lumps, to taste

Heat water to boiling in a kettle. Place the tea in a medium-sized teapot and pour the boiling water over it. Allow the tea to steep for a minute, then add the peppermint, verbena, and sugar. Allow the tea to steep for another minute or so, then pour one glass of tea and return it to the pot. Serve the tea in small glasses.

In Morocco, the tea is poured from a pot that is held in the air so that the tea is aerated; the sound of the pouring tea adds to the pleasure of drinking.

*Available in health food stores.

PROJECT

· · · · · · · · · · · · · · · · · ·

The *mkeka,* or placemat, is one of the seven symbols of Kwanzaa. Placed on the Kwanzaa table, the *mkeka* represents tradition, which is the foundation of all knowledge. In keeping with the idea of *Kujichagulia,* self-determination, the project for the second night of Kwanzaa is to create a family *mkeka.*

Family members should determine which of the *Nguzo Saba* they want to be responsible for and how they will add them to the *mkeka.* They may choose to paint them on, to appliqué them, or to needlepoint or embroider them on. A family decision should be made as to the size of the *mkeka* and of each design, and the fabric that will be used for the background. For large families, each of the *Nguzo Saba* may become a group project. No member is too young or too old to participate. Feel free to incorporate baby footprints, pieces from special garments, and treasured mementos.

Members may work individually, but on one night they should all assemble to put together the *mkeka.* A family member who is good at needlework should be charged with the finishing touches to the *mkeka.* It will rest proudly on the Kwanzaa table next year and be an heirloom for future generations.

FAMILY MKEKA

AND TO MAKE OUR SISTERS' AND BROTHERS' PROBLEMS OUR PROBLEMS AND TO SOLVE THEM TOGETHER. TO BUILD AND MAINTAIN OUR COMMUNITY TOGETHER

THE THIRD NIGHT

UJIMA

COLLECTIVE WORK AND RESPONSIBILITY

He who does not cultivate his field will die of hunger. —Guinean proverb

On the third night of the holiday, as on all nights of Kwanzaa, the celebration begins with the pouring of libation from the *kikombe cha umoja* and the lighting of one of the seven candles of the *kinara.* Tonight, the central black candle of *Umoja,* the first red candle of *Kujichagulia,* and the first green candle of *Ujima* (collective work and responsibility) are lighted. After the candle is lighted, libation is poured or the *kikombe cha umoja* is passed around and thoughts turn to the spirits of those who represented the virtues of *Ujima* in our society.

Tonight is the night we celebrate the spirit of UJIMA (collective work and responsibility).

Tonight and all nights of the year we celebrate the spirits of those who have gone before who represent the values of UJIMA.

We celebrate the spirits of:

Jomo Kenyatta of Kenya
José Carlos do Patrocino of Brazil
Frantz Fanon of Martinique
Fannie Lou Hamer of the United States
_____ (your family selection[s])

and the spirits of all others who worked in our communities bringing neighbors and kin together to achieve greater goals.

Tonight and all other nights, we celebrate the spirits of all those who are here with us.

Tonight and all other nights, we celebrate the spirits of those who are yet to come.

JOMO KENYATTA OF KENYA (1890[?]–1978)

The man who would become Jomo Kenyatta was born to Kikuyu farmers in Ngenda, Kenya, in the 1890s. He underwent traditional colonial mission schooling between 1909 and 1914, and in 1914 was baptized under the name of Johnstone Kamau. He would change this name to Kenyatta in the 1920s as a sign of his increasing political awareness. Active in Kikuyu political organizations, Kenyatta went to London in 1929 as the secretary of the Kikuyu Central Association. In 1931, he returned to London where he studied anthropology at the London School of Economics. In 1938, he published the landmark *Facing Mount Kenya,* a work in which he pioneered the theory of African cultural nationalism. In 1945, he was one of the organizers of the Manchester Pan-African Congress, along with other burgeoning African leaders like Kwame Nkrumah of Ghana.

Upon his return from England, Kenyatta assumed the mantle of leadership of the Kenya African Union. In Kenya, the Mau Mau guerrilla movement was in full force, and in 1952 a state of emergency was declared. In 1953, following a highly controversial trial, Kenyatta was sentenced to seven years imprisonment. It was a time of trouble during which 100 white settlers and more than 13,000 Africans were killed. During the same turbulent years, over 80,000 Kikuyu were placed in detention camps. The emergency lasted until 1960. By its end, land reforms had been enacted and Africans directly elected to the legislative council on a restricted franchise. Kenyatta was released from prison in 1961, but was banned from forming a government. In 1963, however, Kenya became a republic with Jomo Kenyatta as its first president. The *mzee,* or old man, as he was affectionately known in his homeland, ruled the country he so loved until his death in 1978.

Tonight, we salute his spirit. We salute the spirit of the *mzee,* the old man Jomo Kenyatta, for bringing a country out of turmoil into nationhood. We salute him for giving peoples of color throughout the world building blocks to cultural nationalism and showing us that we should all truly work together.

JOSÉ CARLOS DO PATROCINO OF BRAZIL (1853–1905)

Born in the town of Campos in the state of Rio de Janeiro in 1853, José Carlos do Patrocino was the son of a not-so-celibate priest and a black vegetable vendor. Through his own heroic efforts, he was able to go to school and to attend university, where he studied and became a writer, pharmacist, orator, and journalist. He was even a pioneer balloonist! A colossus who bestrode his era of Brazilian history, casting a large shadow, he was nicknamed *O Gigante Negro da Abolição* (The Gigantic Black Man of the Abolitionist Movement). Nothing touching on the struggle of Brazilian blacks for emancipation escaped his hand. Even his detractors conceded that he was a man who was always impassioned and ingenious, and that he expressed himself with a virtuosity of language that was like "a burst of blinding fireworks." A founding member of the Brazilian Academy of Letters, he was also a novelist and a journalist. In keeping with his staunchly abolitionist position, several of his novels dealt with the theme of the evils of slavery. Patrocino was also the founder of the newspaper *A Cidade do Rio de Janeiro (The City of Rio de Janeiro),* which also espoused his abolitionist cause.

When, in 1888, Brazil became the last country in the western hemisphere to abolish slavery, Patrocino's work was done and he went into semioblivion. He died a pauper in 1905 in the Rio de Janeiro that he had so dominated with his personality, but he was not forgotten; over ten thousand people walked in his funeral procession, remembering gratefully the Gigantic Black Man of the Abolitionist Movement.

Tonight, we salute his spirit and the insight of a man who truly understood the principle of *Ujima.* José Carlos do Patrocino, in working to bring freedom to Brazil's children of Africa, knew that in taking responsibility for his brothers and sisters and in helping his community, he was truly helping himself.

FRANTZ FANON OF MARTINIQUE (1925–1961)

Born July 20, 1925, in Fort-de-France, Martinique, Frantz Fanon attended primary school and the prestigious Lycée Schoelcher. One of his teachers was Aimé Césaire, one of the founders of the Negritude movement. As with most students of his era, Fanon, when the time came for higher education, had only one option: schooling in France. Therefore he journeyed to France, where he fought in the French Army during World War II. There, too, he attended medical school in Lyon; he graduated with a degree in psychiatry. In 1952, the year of his graduation, he published the landmark work *Peau Noire, Masques Blancs (Black Skin, White Masks),* a riveting series of observations of black-white relationships.

Fanon's world soon expanded, for in 1953, he was sent to Algeria as director of psychiatric services at Blida-Joinville Hospital. The Algeria to which Fanon journeyed was a land of political upheaval on the verge of a violent overthrow of its colonial masters, the French; it was there that he would find his place as an activist. Fanon published articles in the local press. Expelled from Algeria, he became a member of the press service of the Algerian National Liberation Front in Tunisia.

Profoundly marked by his Algerian experience, Fanon felt at one with the Algerian cause. He saw links between all of the world's oppressed peoples and their fights for freedom. These thoughts would be the catalyst behind his work *Les Damnés de la Terre (The Wretched of the Earth),* in which he outlined strategies for all those seeking to fight for freedom, equality, and dignity, strategies that are as valid today as when they were written over thirty years ago. It would be his last completed work. Fanon died of leukemia in 1961.

Tonight we celebrate the spirit of Frantz Fanon as that of one who understood that the community of oppression is international, transcending nationality and gender, and that oppression can only be overcome by the work of all of us together. We celebrate his works that offer us strategies with which to empower our communities, and through our communities, ourselves.

FANNIE LOU HAMER OF THE UNITED STATES (1917–1977)

 No one who lived through the turbulent years of the Civil Rights Movement in the United States will ever forget the face and the voice of Fannie Lou Hamer. Born in 1917 in Montgomery County, Mississippi, she was the youngest of twenty children born to a family of sharecroppers. Hamer knew firsthand the limitations that the world of Jim Crow placed on the black people of the United States. By the time that she was forty-three years old, when she was about to step out onto the stage of history, she was no stranger to the cotton fields, where she had been working since the age of six. She had been forced to leave school at age thirteen, and she had also been sterilized, compelled, without her knowledge and without her consent, to give up her right to bear children.

In 1962, she attended a rally given by the Student Nonviolent Coordinating Committee, where disenfranchised blacks were asked to volunteer to register to vote. Hamer raised her hand, and after two years of fighting the system, she was finally registered in January 1963. Galvanized, she immediately began helping others to defeat the corrupt system and register to vote. Her activism led her to the vice-chairmanship of the Mississippi Freedom Democrat Party, from there to the Democratic National Convention in Atlantic City, New Jersey, and from there into the minds and consciences of all of America. Her stirring words describing the horrors of racism in her home state of Mississippi and her personal past captured the attention of the nation. A plain speaker who spoke from her heart with fire and feeling, Fannie Lou Hamer crystallized the thoughts of hundreds of thousands of black Americans when she said simply and eloquently, "I'm just sick and tired of being sick and tired."

We celebrate her spirit tonight as one who honored the principle of *Ujima*. Uneducated, poor, and black, she worked from and for her community. She used the tools she had—her homegrown wisdom, her heartfelt eloquence, and her unflagging courage—to change the system for herself and all others like her.

The meal celebrating the Nguzo Saba of Ujima is a bring-a-dish potluck supper for family and friends. All of the dishes on tonight's menu can be packed away and taken elsewhere for a larger communal supper.

Appetizer
GRILLED SHRIMP WITH PILI PILI SAUCE

Salad
ROMAINE SALAD WITH ORANGE AND RADISH

Main Dish
HERBED CHICKEN THIGHS

Vegetables
"STIR-FRIED" BROCCOLI WITH GARLIC
CARROTS WITH GINGER

Starch
SPICY THREE-CHEESE MACARONI AND CHEESE

Dessert
DEEP DISH APPLE COBBLER

Beverage
PINK PARTY PUNCH

GRILLED SHRIMP WITH PILI PILI SAUCE

SERVES 6 TO 8 AS AN APPETIZER

In coastal areas of Western Africa, Brazil, the Caribbean, and the southern United States, shrimp usually are eaten boiled or grilled with a bit of extra zing given by a hot sauce. This recipe grills the shrimp in the broiler and then serves them with an accompanying hot sauce.

½ cup fresh lemon juice
1 clove garlic, minced
1 small onion, minced
Salt and freshly ground black pepper,
    to taste

2 pounds jumbo shrimp, peeled and
    deveined

Preheat the broiler. Combine the lemon juice, garlic, onion, salt, and pepper in a nonreactive bowl. Add the shrimp, cover with plastic wrap, and allow them to marinate in the refrigerator for at least 2 hours.

Remove the shrimp from the marinade, reserving 3 tablespoons of the mixture, and place them on a grilling rack. Cook for 2 to 3 minutes or until they are tender. Serve hot with toothpicks and pili pili sauce.

PILI PILI SAUCE

3 tablespoons reserved shrimp
    marinade (see above)
1 small red bell pepper

¼ teaspoon minced habanero or
    other hot chile, to taste

Mix the ingredients together in the bowl of a blender or food processor and pulse until you have a thin paste. Place the sauce in a small bowl, adjust the seasonings to taste, and serve with the shrimp.

ROMAINE SALAD WITH ORANGE AND RADISH

SERVES 6 TO 8

In my house, no meal is complete without a salad. To keep friends—and myself—from being bored, I vary the salads with new ingredients and new dressings. This salad was inspired by a traditional Moroccan salad, but has the addition of romaine lettuce and a classic vinaigrette with the surprise of a hint of orange juice.

2 small heads romaine lettuce
3 large navel oranges
1 bunch radishes
1½ tablespoons red wine vinegar

5 tablespoons extra-virgin olive oil
Salt and freshly ground black pepper, to taste

Wash the romaine thoroughly, tear it into bite-size pieces, and place it in a large glass salad bowl. Peel the oranges carefully over a small bowl, reserving the juice. Run a sharp knife along the edge of the membrane separating the orange segments and around the each segment. The membrane will come away, leaving an unencumbered orange segment. Add the orange segments to the salad bowl. Squeeze the remaining orange pulp into the bowl with your hands to retain all of the juice. Wash the radishes thoroughly and slice them into rounds, reserving 3 or 4 larger ones to grate for the garnish. Add the radish rounds to the salad bowl.

Prepare a vinaigrette with the remaining ingredients plus 1 tablespoon of the reserved orange juice. Grate the remaining radishes over the salad and drizzle the salad dressing over it. Serve at once.

HERBED CHICKEN THIGHS

••••••••••••
SERVES 6

In all areas of Africa and the diaspora chicken is eaten fried, boiled, baked, sautéed, and roasted. This dish is easy to prepare and a perfect dish for a take-along supper because it tastes as good piping hot from the grill as it does after it has cooled to room temperature. Instead of being fried, the chicken is marinated in lemon juice and olive oil, covered with a crust of herbs, and broiled. Any type of chicken can be cooked this way, but chicken thighs taste best to me. I allow two chicken thighs per person, but size and hunger will determine how many you need.

12 medium-sized chicken thighs
2 tablespoons extra-virgin olive oil
3 tablespoons fresh lemon juice
2 tablespoons dried thyme

1 tablespoon dried oregano
Salt and freshly ground black pepper,
  to taste

Wash the chicken thighs and pat them dry with paper towels. Combine the olive oil, lemon juice, and half of the herbs in a medium-size nonreactive bowl. Add the chicken thighs, making sure that they are well covered with the marinade. Cover the bowl with plastic wrap and refrigerate for 1 hour.

When ready to cook, preheat the broiler, and combine the remaining herbs. Remove the chicken thighs and roll them in the herbs. Place the thighs on a rack in a broiling pan and cook for 5 to 7 minutes on each side or until they are well browned and fully cooked. (No pink chicken, please!) The herbs will be slightly blackened, but the taste will be ambrosial.

NOTE: Extra chicken thighs can be kept uncooked in the marinade for a day or so, or prepared along with the others. If cooked, they can be refrigerated and served at room temperature or sliced into strips and tossed in a mixed or green salad for a great low-cal lunch.

"STIR-FRIED" BROCCOLI WITH GARLIC

SERVES 6 TO 8

This quick way with broccoli is a change from the usual steamed vegetable. Not stir-fried in the traditional Chinese manner (home stoves do not generate enough heat for that), it is actually pan-fried and then briefly steamed. The crunch of the minced bits of garlic and the subtle taste of sesame oil make the combination a sure winner.

2 heads broccoli	4 cloves garlic, cut into thin slivers
1½ tablespoons sesame oil	1 teaspoon water

 Wash the broccoli thoroughly and break it into florets. Peel the stems and cut them crosswise into ½-inch pieces.

Heat the sesame oil in a heavy cast-iron skillet or a wok. When the oil is hot, add the garlic slivers and cook them, stirring rapidly, until they are golden brown and crisp. Be careful. The transition time from crisp to charred is seconds. When ready, remove the garlic slivers and drain them on paper towels. Add the broccoli to the oil and cook it for 3 minutes, then drain off the oil, and add the water. Cover and steam for 2 minutes or until the broccoli is cooked but still crunchy. Sprinkle the broccoli with the reserved garlic bits and serve hot.

CARROTS WITH GINGER

••••••••••••••••••
SERVES 6 TO 8

Root vegetables are winter standbys on the vegetable table. Though many folks whine when served rutabagas and pout over parsnips, one root vegetable that generally meets with universal approval is carrots. Here, they're simply cooked in a little orange juice with a bit of ginger and freshly ground nutmeg to give them more character.

1 bunch carrots (with the green
   tops, if possible)
1 thumb-sized piece of fresh ginger,
   scraped and minced

½ cup fresh orange juice
Salt, freshly ground black pepper, and
   freshly grated nutmeg, to taste
1 tablespoon butter

Wash and scrape the carrots, and cut them into ½-inch rounds. Place the carrots in a medium-sized saucepan. Add the ginger and the orange juice. Cover and cook over moderate heat for 10 minutes or until the carrots are fork-tender. Drain the carrots, reserving the cooking liquid, and season them to taste.

Melt the butter in a small saucepan, add the reserved cooking liquid, and stir until combined. Drizzle the butter and orange juice over the carrots, and serve hot.

SPICY THREE-CHEESE
MACARONI AND CHEESE

•••••••••••••
SERVES 6

No winter potluck supper table would be complete without a casserole of macaroni and cheese. Traditionally, the dish is prepared with Cheddar cheese, American cheese, or even Velveeta. It has also been known to be the delicious final resting place for more than one pack-

age of the infamous government cheese that is handed out to the less fortunate. In this recipe, the traditional Cheddar-style cheese-flavored dish meets up with the African-American love for things hot and well seasoned with the addition of pepper Jack, a bit of Parmesan, and a dash of hot sauce.

1½ cups medium elbow macaroni
2 tablespoons unsalted butter
2 tablespoons flour
¾ cup milk
¾ cup freshly grated extra-sharp Cheddar cheese
½ cup freshly grated pepper Jack cheese

¼ cup freshly grated Parmesan cheese
1 teaspoon hot sauce, or to taste
Salt and freshly ground black pepper, to taste
¼ cup fine dry bread crumbs

Preheat the oven to 350 degrees. Lightly grease a 1½-quart baking dish. Cook the macaroni according to package directions until tender but still firm. Drain it and place it in the greased casserole dish. Melt the butter over medium heat in a small saucepan and whisk in the flour. Cook for about 2 minutes or until the mixture is thick and pasty. Gradually drizzle in the milk, whisking constantly, and cook for 7 to 8 minutes, or until the sauce has thickened. Remove the sauce from the heat but keep it warm.

Reserve 1 tablespoon of each of the cheeses in a small bowl. Add the remaining cheese to the white sauce and stir in until smooth. (You may have to return the pan to the stove over low heat to melt the cheeses.) Add the hot sauce and season to taste. Pour the sauce over the macaroni in the casserole and stir it well to make sure that everything is well mixed. Add the bread crumbs to the 3 tablespoons reserved cheese, mix them well, and sprinkle the crumb-cheese mixture over the top of the macaroni. Bake for 35 to 40 minutes, or until hot, bubbly, and lightly browned on the top. Serve hot.

BASIC PIE CRUST

....

MAKES 1 (8- OR 9-INCH) SINGLE CRUST PIE SHELL

This is the holiday, so only the true pie purist will tell if you cheat a bit and use a prepared pie crust or a pie crust mix. (If so, select the best!) However, for the pie crust purists among us, here's a recipe for a flaky basic pie crust.

1 cup flour

½ teaspoon salt

⅓ cup chilled lard or shortening

2 or 3 tablespoons cold water

Mix the flour and salt in a medium-sized bowl. Cut the lard or shortening into the mixture with a pastry blender or 2 knives until it has the consistency of cornmeal. Slowly, add 2 tablespoons of the water to the mixture, using a fork to mix it in until it becomes a dough. If the dough seems too crumbly, add the remaining water a bit at a time (but remember the trick to a flaky pie crust is to handle it as litle as possible). Flatten the dough into a disk, wrap it in wax paper, and refrigerate for at least 30 minutes. When ready to use, remove the dough from the refrigerator and roll it out on a floured surface.

DEEP DISH APPLE COBBLER

SERVES 6 TO 8

Cobblers appear on African-Atlantic lunch and dinner tables, at church suppers, and outdoor barbecues. They are prepared from whatever fresh fruit is handy, and when there's no fresh fruit, they're even occasionally prepared from dried or preserved fruits. This cobbler is a winter staple that uses apples, which are usually readily available.

12 medium-sized Granny Smith or
    other cooking apples
1 cup packed light brown sugar
1 teaspoon fresh lemon juice
1 tablespoon cold butter

1 teaspoon powdered cinnamon
1 teaspoon freshly grated nutmeg
1 single 8- or 9-inch single unbaked
    pie crust (page 82)

 Preheat the oven to 375 degrees. Generously butter a 1½-quart baking dish.

Wash the apples, peel them, core them, and slice them lengthwise into ¼-inch slices. Place the slices, along with 1 cup of the brown sugar and the lemon juice in the baking dish. Dot the apples with the butter and season them with the cinnamon and nutmeg.

Roll the pie crust dough out on a floured surface. Cut out a circle the size of the top of the baking dish. Trim the scraps and place them in with the apples, sugar, lemon juice, and seasonings. Place the crust on top of the apples, covering the top of the baking dish. Seal it to the top of the dish, and flute the edges by pincing them between your thumb and forefinger. Slash two or three steam vents in the crust with a sharp knife. Bake for 30 minutes, or until the crust is golden brown. Serve hot. Traditionally, cobbler is served in small bowls with a bit of crust, the warm apples, and their liquid. Those who want a real treat can top it with a bit of vanilla ice cream and a dusting of brown sugar.

PINK PARTY PUNCH

SERVES 6 TO 8

All manner of beverages turn up at parties and potluck suppers, from doctored-up pitchers of Kool-Aid to fancy minted lemonades. This pink party punch is a crowd pleaser that is perfect for the underage set, those who are designated drivers, and those who just plain don't drink alcohol.

1 package frozen strawberries in syrup

2 tablespoons fresh lime juice

2 cups fresh orange juice

2 tablespoons grenadine

4 cups ginger ale

Place the frozen strawberries in the bowl of a blender or food processor and blend until they are liquid. Place the strawberries and all of the remaining ingredients in a large pitcher, add the ginger ale and ice, stir well, and serve.

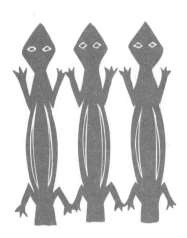

PROJECT

••••••••••••••••••••••

The proverb selected for this the third night of Kwanzaa says, "He who does not cultivate his field will die of hunger." These fields are not only literal but also metaphorical. Tonight is the time to consider cultivating the fields of our communities around the country and around the world. Hunger, the second part of the proverb, is an all too real bogeyman in many of our communities, affecting thousands of men, women, and children.

Tonight's project is to work to alleviate that hunger. In creating your own potluck supper tonight to share with family and friends, ask each invited guest to bring along a second dish to be shared with the homeless shelter, AIDS hospice, senior citizen's center, or other group of your choice. When you go to bring the dishes, take the children of the family along and explain to them why you are doing this. Make this journey not simply a once-a-year Kwanzaa excursion, but a part of your weekly or monthly routines. In that way, we can pass along not only the tales told around the *kinara* each night of Kwanzaa, but also establish and perpetuate the tradition of collective work and responsibility that underlie the *Nguzo Saba* of this third night: *Ujima*.

FAMILY NOTES

TO BUILD AND MAINTAIN OUR OWN STORES,

AND TO PROFIT FROM THEM TOGETHER.

THE FOURTH NIGHT

UJAMAA

COOPERATIVE ECONOMICS

It is no shame to work for money. —*Ashanti proverb*

On the fourth night of Kwanzaa as on all other nights of the holiday, the celebration begins with the question *Habari gani?* The answer is *Ujamaa* (cooperative economics). The asking of the Kwanzaa question is followed by the pouring of libation from the *kikombe cha umoja* and the lighting of the candles of the *kinara.* Tonight, first the central black candle of *Umoja,* then the first red candle of *Kujichagulia,* then the first green candle of *Ujima* are lighted. The second red candle, the candle of *Ujamaa* is lighted for the first time. After the candles are lighted, libation is poured or the *kikombe cha umoja* is passsed around and thoughts turn to the spirits of those who represented the virtues of *Ujamaa* in our communities.

Tonight is the night we celebrate the spirit of UJAMAA (cooperative economics).

Tonight and all nights of the year, we celebrate the spirits of those who have gone before who represent the values of UJAMAA.

We celebrate the spirits of:

Julius Nyerere of Tanzania
Natalino José do Nascimento of Brazil
Violetta Symphort of Guadeloupe
John Merrick of the United States
_____ (your family selection[s])

and the spirits of all others who worked in our communities to visualize, establish, create, and nurture economic organizations that enabled all of us to prosper.

Tonight and all nights, we celebrate the spirits of all those who are here with us.

Tonight and all other nights, we celebrate the spirits of those who are yet to come.

JULIUS NYERERE OF TANZANIA (1922–)

Julius Nyerere is the only one of our ancestor spirits who still walks the earth. I have designated him as an ancestor spirit for he truly is the ancestor of much of today's political theory and because his powerful doctrine of cooperative economics is one that we all need to survive. He has completely retired from politics.

Born the son of a chief in northwestern Tanganyika, Julius Nyerere was educated at government schools in that country. He received his degree in education from Makerere College in Uganda and taught for several years in Tanganyika. He journeyed to Edinburgh, Scotland to study, received his M.A. degree from Edinburgh University in 1952, and returned to Tanganyika to teach. In 1954, he was a founding member of the Tanganyika African National Union. By 1955, he had abandoned teaching to devote his full-time efforts to campaigning for independence and to political organizing. He moved up the political ranks, and when Tanganyika became independent in December 1961, he became the country's first prime minister. He resigned this post six weeks later over political differences to devote himself completely to TANU. In October of the following year, however, when Tanganyika became a republic, he returned as the country's first president. He subsequently became the first president of Tanzania, the union of Tanganyika and Zanzibar, in 1965.

Nyerere was an innovative statesman whose policies stressed rural development for his country and the need for all to work together. Living simply, without pomp and ceremony, Nyerere focused on his belief that in order for us to develop and prosper, we must depend on ourselves, on our own resources, and on our own abilities.

Tonight, we salute the spirit of Nyerere, showing us all ways to a better economic future. We salute him for teaching us that our past and our future are in each of us. In order to better ourselves, we must better each other. Finally, we salute him for making us all truly learn the meaning of the word *harambee* (let us pull together!), for without it we have no future.

NATALINO JOSÉ DO NASCIMENTO OF BRAZIL (1905–1975)

 Most who experience the thunder of the drums, the volume of the music, and the tidal-wave crowds of hip-shaking samba dancers that make up Carnival in Rio de Janeiro, Brazil, would not think that the festival that has become one of the world's best known has its origins in neighborhood organizations. Yet that is really what the Rio's famous samba schools are.

One of the early heroes of Rio's samba schools was Natalino José do Nascimento, known simply as Natal.

Natal experienced the extremes of poverty that are all too common for those living in the *favelas* or shanty towns that dot the hillsides over Rio de Janeiro. Where there is poverty, there are dreams. Where there are dreams and no money, there are lotteries. Following an accident that resulted in his arm being amputated, and with no trade of his own to ply, Natal became a numbers man for the Brazilian clandestine numbers game: the *Jogo de Bicho* (Animal Game) in 1928. Natal was tough and soon became the virtual uncrowned king of his neighborhood. Unlike most of his fellow *bicheros,* or numbers bankers, Natal did not squander his money. Instead, he financed his samba school, Portela, and donated large amounts of money for the construction of recreational and athletic facilities in his neighborhood. He himself declared his Robin Hood–like theory of life: "Some of my money went to my family, some to the [samba] school, and the rest I would give to people who needed it."

Tonight we salute the spirit of Natal, not for the life he led nor for the way he earned his living. Tonight we salute the spirit of Natal because, despite his human faults, he understood the virtue of *Ujamaa.* He worked to build his community and to offer more opportunities to those who lived in it. Rooted in the reality of his life, he nonetheless understood the proverb that states: "Through others I am somebody."

VIOLETTA SYMPHORT OF GUADELOUPE (19??–1991)

Africa lives on in the Western Hemisphere in many guises. There are secret societies, clubs, and coming-of-age rituals. We have our *sousous* and our box hands as alternative savings institutions, and our burial societies as alternative insurance companies.

The Société Saint Laurent of Guadeloupe is a society formed by the cooks of Guadeloupe as a self-help organization, collecting small amounts of money from members to assure them that when they are ill or unable to work, they will be taken care of. The Société also assures members that they will have a proper funeral. The immediate past president of this Société was a woman known as Violetta Symphort.

Born on the island of Guadeloupe to a culinary family, Violetta Symphort was destined to cook. Learning from her mother and relatives, over the years she developed a mastery of the secrets of the classic Creole cuisine that is so much a part of Guadeloupe. She learned to prepare the *court bouillons* and the *blaffs,* to make the *matété* and the *mignan.* Slowly, she worked her way through the kitchens of the island and from the kitchens into her own restaurant. Her restaurant grew and prospered, and she grew in importance to the community, becoming a virtual culinary ambassadress for her country.

Her personal financial success was assured, yet she retained membership in the Sociéte Saint Laurent. When she died, she was given a funeral in keeping with her Roman Catholic faith and the ceremonies of the Société Saint Laurent.

We salute the spirit of Violetta Symphort tonight as one person who never forgot her origins. We recognize her and the Société that she headed as a link with our past, and the cooperative economics that it practiced as a signpost for our future.

JOHN MERRICK OF THE UNITED STATES (1859–1919)

Born into slavery near Clinton, North Carolina, in 1859, John Merrick grew up at a time when most black folk were concerned with getting from day to day and had no thoughts of saving for the future or providing for their burial and those they would leave behind. During the period of enslavement, these things were taken care of by the masters and, following Emancipation, times in most cases were too hard for folk to worry. Tradition had it that widows and orphans were helped by their families aided by their communities. Collections were taken up and saucer burials, where each attendee dropped a few pitiful coins into a saucer to aid in the proper burial of the deceased, were the norm.

John Merrick knew the hard times as well. At age twelve, he was sent to work as a laborer in a brick yard in Chapel Hill and there began to learn a trade that would stand him in good stead. He also learned how to read, write, and calculate. After six years at the brick yard, his family moved to Raleigh where he again found work as a brick mason, but jobs became scarce and he had to find other work. He did, as a bootblack in a barber shop. While he shined shoes, he learned the trade of barbering and soon became a partner and eventually the owner of a barbershop in the county seat of the newly created county of Durham, North Carolina. Merrick's fortunes continued to improve; the one shop became five barbershops, and he began to invest in real estate in the town, which grew rapidly as people poured into it to work in the tobacco factories.

Merrick's personal wealth grew along with the town, but he never lost touch with his customers or with his desire to work for community betterment. No one knows exactly why Merrick and six of his friends decided to begin an industrial insurance business, but in 1899 the North Carolina Mutual and Provident Association was incorporated by the State of North Carolina. The company's motto, "Merciful to All," speaks more to the desires of Merrick and the other founders than anything else. A portion of the company's proceeds was to be turned over to the

Colored Orphan Asylum in Oxford, North Carolina. The company that Merrick began has been a pioneer in providing mortgages for African-Americans around the country, in aiding the creation of new businesses, and in generally helping other African-Americans keep their dreams alive. It lives on even though he died in 1919.

Tonight, we salute John Merrick for his business acumen, for his ability to triumph over adversity, to rise and thrive and prosper. We salute him for knowing that no African-American business is truly successful unless it helps us all learn and succeed. We salute him as one who truly knew the meaning of *Ujamaa* and who used it to help us all grow.

The menu celebrating the Nguzo Saba of Ujamaa is
a formal meal for business networking. It can be used during
Kwanzaa as a meal for friends to come together
to discuss business plans and ideas, or at any time of the year
to entertain business contacts and clients.

Appetizer

BROILED GRAPEFRUIT WITH RUM

Salad

ENDIVE WITH PEARS AND ROQUEFORT

Main Dish

PECAN-COATED ROAST LOIN OF PORK WITH BAKED PEACHES

Condiment

PEACH APRICOT CHUTNEY

Vegetables

GARLIC/SESAME STRING BEANS

BAKED POTATOES WITH SPICED YOGURT

Dessert

SAUTÉED BANANAS WITH RUM RAISIN SAUCE

Beverage

CARIBBEAN SORREL

BROILED GRAPEFRUIT WITH RUM

•••••••••••••
SERVES 6

This appetizer is simple, but it makes a perfectly delicious opening statement. With the addition of rum and a bit of brown sugar, the ordinary grapefruit half is transformed into something that signals a festive meal to come.

3 ruby red grapefruit   ¼ cup rum, or to taste
¼ cup packed dark brown sugar

Preheat the broiler. Cut the grapefruit in half and separate each individual segment by running a sharp knife around each small triangular section inside the membrane. Lift the sections out slightly, and then return them.

When all of the grapefruit segments have been cut, sprinkle a bit of brown sugar on each one and drizzle on the rum. Place the grapefruit in a baking dish that will fit into your broiler and then broil them for 5 minutes, or until the sugar has melted and the grapefruit halves are slightly browned on the top. Serve hot.

ENDIVE WITH PEARS
AND ROQUEFORT

SERVES 6

The combination of Belgian endive, ripe Anjou pears, and Roquefort, the king of the blue cheeses, is just ambrosial. This recipe mixes them together with a dash of a classic vinaigrette for a winter salad that's absolutely elegant.

3 small heads Belgian endive
2 medium-sized firm, ripe Anjou
   pears
⅓ cup crumbled Roquefort cheese*
¼ teaspoon Dijon mustard
⅔ cup olive oil

3 tablespoons red wine vinegar
1 tablespoon balsamic vinegar
Pinch sugar
Salt and freshly ground black pepper,
   to taste

Wash the endive, separate it into leaves, and pat them dry with absorbent paper. Wash the pears, core them, and cut them into thin lengthwise slices. Arrange the endive and the pear slices on 6 individual salad plates and sprinkle them with the crumbled Roquefort cheese.

Prepare the dressing by mixing the mustard, olive oil, vinegars, sugar, salt, and pepper together in a small bowl. Drizzle it over the salads. Serve at once.

The salad dressing may be prepared in advance and kept in the refrigerator until needed. If so, whisk well before using.

* If you cannot find Roquefort, you may substitute any good blue cheese.

PECAN-COATED ROAST LOIN OF PORK WITH BAKED PEACHES

SERVES 8

The traditional roast pork is given a southern accent with a crust of well-seasoned crushed pecans. Thinly sliced pork loin with a slathering of the chutney makes perfect sandwiches to take to work or school.

4 pounds boneless loin of pork
¼ cup olive oil
2 teaspoons powdered sage
1 teaspoon dried thyme
1 teaspoon minced garlic
Salt and freshly ground black pepper,
    to taste

1 tablespoon packed dark brown
    sugar
¼ pound shelled pecan halves
Baked Peaches (page 98)

Rub the pork loin with olive oil, making sure that it is well covered. Combine the sage, thyme, garlic, salt, pepper, and brown sugar in the bowl of a food processor or blender and pulse until you have a thick paste. You may have to add a drizzle of olive oil to get it started. Slather the paste all over the pork loin, cover it with plastic wrap, and refrigerate it overnight.

Preheat the oven to 400 degrees. Place the pecans in the bowl of a food processor or blender and pulse until they are finely chopped. Roll the pork loin in the crushed pecans and place it in a roasting pan. Make a tent of aluminum foil and arrange it over the pork loin, covering the nuts completely so that they won't char.

Roast for 30 minutes; then lower the heat to 350 degrees and continue to roast. After 1 hour and 20 minutes, remove the aluminum foil and continue to roast until the pork is done, approximately 20 minutes more. Serve hot with baked peaches.

BAKED PEACHES

••••••••••••

SERVES 8

These savory peaches are the perfect acompaniment to winter roasts. If there are only a few guests at the table, you may wish to serve a bit of the peach-apricot chutney in each of the baked peaches. If the guests are more numerous, serve the peaches as a side dish with the meat.

8 canned freestone peach halves (the number varies from can to can, regardless of weight, so check!)

2 tablespoons packed dark brown sugar

Freshly grated nutmeg

After the roast has cooked for 1 hour, place the peach halves around it in the bottom of the roasting pan. Sprinkle the peaches with 2 tablespoons brown sugar and a grinding of nutmeg. When the roast is ready, they will be done. Serve hot with the roast.

PEACH APRICOT CHUTNEY

MAKES ABOUT 2 CUPS

I think that roasted meats always cry for a condiment; my preference is for a homemade chutney. This chutney uses canned peaches and dried apricots; the peaches complement the baked peaches that accompany the pork loin, and the habanero chile adds zing.

½ pound dried apricots
6 canned freestone peach halves, drained
⅛ teaspoon minced habanero or other hot chile, or to taste
1 (1-inch) piece fresh ginger, scraped

Pinch powdered cloves (grind them yourself for the best flavor)
1 cup sugar
1 cup cider vinegar

In a medium-sized bowl, soak the apricots in water to cover for 1 hour. Drain the apricots, reserving ¼ cup of the soaking liquid. Place the apricots and the reserved liquid, the peach halves, chile, ginger, and cloves in the bowl of a food processor or blender and pulse until you have a thick paste.

Place the paste in a nonreactive saucepan and stir in the sugar and vinegar. Bring to a boil over medium heat, then lower the heat and cook until the mixture reaches a jamlike texture, stirring occasionally to make sure that the chutney does not stick to the bottom of the saucepan or scorch. It will take about 40 minutes, but cooking time will vary. Just keep cooking until you have the correct consistency.

Spoon the chutney into scalded glass jars and refrigerate if you are using it within a week. If you're preparing a large batch to share with friends or to store, process according to proper canning methods.

GARLIC/SESAME STRING BEANS

SERVES 6 TO 8

Most folk would think that this vegetable dish has an Asian overtone. Perhaps it does, but many think sesame seeds are African in origin, so I guess we could stake a claim as well. In any case, this recipe gives a new twist to plain old string beans.

2 pounds fresh, unblemished string beans

2 tablespoons unsalted butter

1 tablespoon minced garlic, to taste

2 tablespoons toasted sesame seeds

Bring 4 cups of water to a boil in a medium-sized saucepan. Wash the string beans and cut off the stem ends with a paring knife. When the water has reached a rolling boil, plunge the string beans into the water and allow them to cook for 5 to 7 minutes or until they are cooked but firm and crisp. Remove them from the heat, drain them, and reserve.

Heat the butter in a medium-sized skillet. When it is foamy, add the garlic and the sesame seeds and cook, stirring constantly, until the garlic is lightly browned. Add the string beans and continue to cook, stirring constantly, until the string beans are completely coated with the garlic and sesame seeds. Serve hot.

BAKED POTATOES
WITH SPICED YOGURT

••••••••••••
SERVES 8

Just about everyone loves baked potatoes. Most of us add butter and/or sour cream, but this recipe offers a healthier twist. The spiced yogurt is delicious enough that you might just want to eat it with sliced vegetable sticks as a snack by itself. These potatoes can be popped into the oven along with the pork loin, making them not only healthful, but also energy-efficient. The spicy yogurt can be prepared several hours or even a few days ahead.

8 medium-sized baking potatoes
1 cup plain yogurt
1 tablespoon minced fresh cilantro
   (leaf coriander)

3 scallions, chopped, including
   2 inches of the green part
½ teaspoon powdered cumin

Scrub the potatoes and prick them with a fork. After the pork loin has been cooking for half an hour, arrange the potatoes on the oven racks in the remaining space. They will be ready at the same time as the pork loin.

While the potatoes are baking, mix the yogurt, cilantro, scallions, and cumin together in a small bowl, cover with plastic wrap, and place it in the refrigerator for at least 1 hour.

When the potatoes are ready, split them open and serve each one with a heaping dollop of the spiced yogurt. You won't even miss the butter and sour cream.

SAUTÉED BANANAS WITH RUM RAISIN SAUCE

••••••••••••
SERVES 8

The sweet, slightly starchy taste of bananas just seems to go perfectly with the molasses taste of Caribbean dark rum. In this dessert the ingredients blend to form a dessert that can be a showy finish to any meal.

½ cup dark raisins
¾ cup dark Caribbean rum
8 firm, ripe bananas
4 tablespoons (½ stick) unsalted
   butter

¼ cup packed dark brown sugar
Freshly grated nutmeg

Combine the raisins and the rum in a small bowl and let stand for 30 minutes. Peel the bananas and slice them in half lengthwise.

In a large heavy skillet heat the butter until foamy and add the bananas, round side down. Cook for 2 to 3 minutes on each side, turning them carefully so that they do not break. Remove them from the frying pan, arrange them on a serving platter, and keep them warm.

In the same skillet, mix the rum and raisins with the butter remaining in the pan, brown sugar, and nutmeg and heat until warmed through. (At this point you may wish to flambé the rum by carefully lighting it with a match.) Pour the rum raisin sauce over the bananas and serve at once. For a super special dessert, these bananas can be served with vanilla or banana ice cream.

CARIBBEAN SORREL

....

MAKES 1 QUART

It wouldn't be Christmas in the Caribbean without the deep pink beverage known as sorrel. Prepared from the pods of a red flowering plant of the hibiscus family, sorrel is also drunk in West Africa. Senegalese folk savor it as well, but without the additional spices, and call it BISSAP ROUGE.

When purchasing sorrel, be careful: You don't want the green leaf known by the French as sorrel; you're looking for dried reddish brown pods. You can find it in health food stores and in Caribbean markets year-round. In the Caribbean, adults drink their holiday sorrel mixed with liberal doses of whatever local rum is their preferred brand. You can drink yours plain or mixed with rum as well. Select a good rum from the English-speaking Caribbean, like Mount Gay, Cockspur, or Appleton.

2 heaping cups dried sorrel pods
5 whole cloves
1 tablespoon grated orange zest
1 (2-inch) stick cinnamon
¼ teaspoon freshly grated nutmeg

1½ tablespoons grated fresh ginger
1 quart boiling water
1 cup superfine sugar, to taste
Several grains uncooked white rice

Place the sorrel pods, cloves, orange zest, cinnamon, nutmeg, and ginger in a large crock or heavy bowl. Pour the boiling water over them and allow the mixture to steep for 24 hours.

When ready, strain the sorrel and add the sugar, stirring well. Pour the sorrel into a scalded quart jar that can be loosely capped and add the rice. (There are lots of theories about what it does, but all agree that the best reason to add it is that it's traditional.) Allow the jar to remain in a cool, dark place for 2 days or longer, then serve. This sorrel is strong and should be served diluted: half sorrel, half water. Whether or not you choose to add rum is strictly up to you.

PROJECT

The desire for families to communicate with each other at special times is not one created by Hallmark. The basic human need to share news, good wishes, and hopes with family and friends is something that is universal, especially when our families are increasingly separated and scattered.

The project for the fourth night of Kwanzaa is to maintain contact with friends and family near and far by means of your own family-created notecards. With a bit of *Kuumba,* creativity, you can transform a blank piece of paper into your own special message. Get out the crayons, colored pencils, glue gun, and sparkles. Dust off those rubber stamps and stickers, and try to remember where you put the ink pad. This is the time to think about making collages from those second prints of family vacation photographs that you keep getting from the photo store, and those magazines that have been sitting in the corner for too long. Put those verses you've been keeping in your head and those you've written on scraps of paper that are scattered around the house to good use. Sit around the kitchen table and snip, clip, and create. Who knows, your cards may be so good that they'll be the start of a family enterprise. What better example of *Ujamaa* can you think of?

FAMILY NOTES

FAMILY NOTES

THE FIFTH NIGHT

NIA

PURPOSE

Before shooting, one must aim. — *Ethiopian proverb*

On the fifth night of Kwanzaa, as on all other nights of the holiday, the celebration begins with the question *Habari gani?* The answer is *Nia* (purpose). The asking of the Kwanzaa question is followed by the lighting of the candles of the *kinara* and the pouring of libation from the *kikombe cha umoja*. Tonight, the second green candle, the candle of *Nia*, is lighted for the first time. After the candles are lighted, libation is poured or the *kikombe cha umoja* is passed around, and thoughts turn to the spirits of those who represented the virtues of *Nia*.

Tonight is the night we celebrate the spirit of NIA (purpose).

Tonight and all nights of the year, we celebrate the spirits of those who have gone before who represent the values of NIA.

We celebrate the spirits of:

> Abla Poku of the Baoule of the Côte d'Ivoire
> Maria Escolástica da Conceição Nazaré of Brazil
> Toussaint L'Ouverture of Haiti
> Thurgood Marshall of the United States
> _____ (your family selection[s]),

and the spirits of all others who worked, nurtured, and sacrificed so that all of us remember the traditional greatness of our ancestors, a legacy that we must nourish and cherish.

Tonight and all nights, we celebrate the spirits of all those who are here with us.

Tonight and all other nights, we celebrate the spirits of those who are yet to come.

ABLA POKU OF THE BAOULE OF THE CÔTE D'IVOIRE (EIGHTEENTH CENTURY)

Born in the West African region between the Volta and the Bandama Rivers in the early part of the eighteenth century, Abla Poku was royal on both her mother's and her father's side of the family. Although of royal birth, she did not have an easy childhood, and her young years were punctuated with the turmoil that marked the eighteenth century among the Akan peoples: wars of succession, the sack of Kumasi by Ebri Moro, the murders of many of her family, and her own exile. Poku's position as potential Queen Mother (an important role in Akan society) made her a pawn in the quarrels over the throne.

No one knows how she found the land to which she led her partisans. Some say that she found it during her early exile. But she led an exodus of thousands of Ashanti-Asabou nobles, their vassals, and households, on a trek that would take them westward. Along the way, the fleeing nobles were aided by villagers and townspeople who joined the caravan, swelling their numbers. It seemed that the entire group was doomed when they reached the banks of the Komoé River in today's Côte d'Ivoire; there, the size of the river made passage impossible.

Legend has it that on the riverbanks, Queen Poku offered her only child to the waters to ensure the safe passage of her people. Uttering the words *Baa-ouli* (the child is dead), the moment of a mother's supreme sacrifice for the good of her people lives on in the new name of the people—*Baoule*. Poku and her sacrifice established a new kingdom in which the Akan matrilineal system of government and the Agoua royal house were assured. When she died in 1760 at Niamonou near what would become the capital of the Baoule kingdom, she had left her mark forever of the history of her people.

We salute the spirit of Queen Abla Poku this evening for her leadership and vision. We honor her for her sense of purpose, her clear focus, and her willingness to offer the supreme maternal sacrifice for the survival of her people.

MARIA ESCOLÁSTICA DA CONCEIÇÃO NAZARÉ OF BRAZIL
(1894–1986)

 Born on February 10, only six years after the formal abolition of slavery in Brazil, Maria Escolástica da Conceição Nazaré was a child with a destiny. Descended from Africans who hailed from the Nigerian town of Abeokuta, she was the great-granddaughter of one of the women who brought the African religion of the Yoruba people to Brazil, where it would evolve into the rite that is known today as Candomblé. Initiated at the age of eight months, she would become the spiritual leader of her religious house, Gantois, at twenty-eight. Born at a time when the religion of her ancestors was reviled as "The Religion of the Blacks" and equated with satanism, she would live to be consulted by statesmen and courted by movie stars, praised in songs written by famous composers, and treated as the uncrowned queen of Salvador da Bahia, Brazil.

A votary of *orixa* of love, coquetry, and rivers known in Brazil as Oxum, Maria Escolástica da Conceição Nazaré became affectionately known through Brazil and beyond its borders as Mae Menininha (Little Girl.) Her fame came from her goodness and her strict adherence to the traditions of her religion. She was intransigent on the subject of the respect that she demanded and commanded for her religion. Candomblé grew during the sixty-four years that Mae Menininha reigned from a religion persecuted by the police and assailed in newspaper editorials to become one of the most potent cultural forces for the betterment of blacks in the history of Brazil.

Mae Menininha was at the forefront of this evolution. Always open to true discussion with all, her willingness to discuss, but not compromise, to lead, yet not terrorize, and to teach, yet not proselytize, made her, in the terms of one newspaper article, "the virtual Pope of Candomblé." Those who had the honor of sitting at her feet (as I did) knew that they had been in the presence of true saintliness and greatness. When she died in 1986, the City of Salvador da Bahia de Todos os Santos mourned her passing. She was given a state funeral which was attended by all from governors to dressmakers, writers to dockworkers, street vendors to singing stars. Shops closed, the radio played mourning dirges, and her funeral occupied the television. She was Bahia's queen and her equal will not again be soon seen.

Tonight we salute the spirit of Mae Menininha of Gantois for her goodness and her greatness. We salute her for her purpose and her leadership, for standing forth and standing firm, and for knowing that the gentle constant force of a river will wear down rock.

TOUSSAINT L'OUVERTURE OF HAITI (1743–1803)

 Toussaint Bréda was born as a slave on the Bréda plantation in the French colony of Saint Domingue. Some say that he was the grandson of a Rada chef of Dahomey who was captured as a slave. As a child, he was frail, but determined, and set about building his endurance so that by the time that he was twelve he was a formidable athlete. Even at age sixty, he rode 125 miles daily on horseback with ease and was known as "the Centaur of the Savannahs." He was not handsome, but he had character, personality, and intellect that set him above other men long before he entered the political scene.

Toussaint worked on the plantation as steward of livestock and then as slave coachman, positions that honed his skills at management and reinforced his abilities to lead. He could also read, no mean accomplishment during the troubled times at the end of the eighteenth century in Saint Domingue. Toussaint Bréda joined the revolution late and as an "old" man—he was forty-five—and he advanced rapidly to the top ranks.

The deeds of the Haitian Revolution are complex and bloody, and affect the history of that land even today; yet they were the crucible for the birthplace of greatness. Toussaint Bréda became known to the world as Toussaint L'Ouverture (the Opening) for his military ability to open the ranks of his enemies. He rose to the forefront of history through his leadership, his military genius, and his intellect. Fighting for his freedom and the freedom of others like him, he cut a swath through history. In his ruling of Saint Domingue, he freed his people, pacified the country, began rebuilding agriculture, and governed fairly. It was not to last. Captured by the treachery of Napoléon Bonaparte, Toussaint L'Ouverture was taken to France and held without trial in a prison in the French Alps, where he died in exile on April 27, 1803.

We salute the indomitable spirit of Toussaint L'Ouverture tonight as one whose sense of purpose changed a world. We salute him as one of the founders of the first independent black nation in this hemisphere and as one who knew the price of liberty. We salute his spirit tonight on this night of purpose for his purpose and vision in saying to the world, "In overthrowing me, you have cut down in Saint Domingue only the trunk of the tree of liberty. It will spring up again by the roots, for they are numerous and deep."

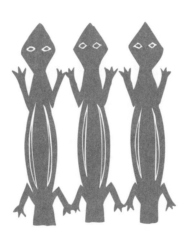

THURGOOD MARSHALL OF THE UNITED STATES (1908–1993)

Thurgood Marshall was born in Baltimore, Maryland, in 1908, the grandson of an African-born slave. His father was a steward in a white country club and his mother taught in segregated schools. Educated at Lincoln University in Pennsylvania and at Howard University Law School, Marshall entered private law practice following his graduation.

His interest, though, was in the growing Civil Rights movement, and at the same time that he was in law practice, he worked for the National Association for the Advancement of Colored People (NAACP). By 1938, he had become the organization's chief counsel. During the years from 1938 until 1961, when he was appointed to the United States Court of Appeals, he worked on numerous civil rights cases, including ones that lead to the admission of the first African-American student to the University of Missouri Law School, the desegregation of interstate passenger carriers in Virginia, and the landmark 1954 *Brown* v. (the Topeka) *Board of Education,* one of the first steps on the road to school desegregation.

Marshall was appointed associate justice of the United States Supreme Court by President Lyndon B. Johnson in 1967. He sat on the Supreme Court until his retirement in 1991. Known among his friends for his wicked wit, when asked the reason for his retirement from the Supreme Court, Marshall simply replied, "Why? Because I'm old!" He *was* old, but his opinions in the area of civil rights were trenchant and timely.

We salute the spirit of Thurgood Marshall this evening because he represents singleness of purpose. Once his focus was aimed at seeing that African-Americans, and indeed *all* Americans, were not deprived of their civil rights, he persevered. His sound judgment and wisdom were tempered with humor and never failed him. He pursued his goals with a sureness of focus and a tenacity of conviction that never flagged. We salute the spirit of Thurgood Marshall this evening, for he truly epitomized *Nia.*

The menu celebrating NIA is a meal reminding us
of our ancestors' American presence. It is a meal of the
foods of adversity, as transformed by a people
whose greatness could not be destroyed.

Appetizer
SAUTÉED PECANS

Salad
WILTED WINTER SALAD WITH JERUSALEM ARTICHOKES

Main Dish
ROAST CHICKEN

Condiment
SPICY VINEGAR

Vegetables
BAKED SWEET POTATOES
HOME-STYLE COLLARDS WITH SPICY VINEGAR

Dessert
HOLIDAY GINGERBREAD WITH MOLASSES WHIPPED CREAM

Beverage
EGGNOG

SAUTÉED PECANS

•••••••••••
SERVES 8

Pecans were a part of the lives of many of our ancestors in the South. In some areas, they were so plentiful that they simply fell from the trees. They are still readily available, and many families receive a sackful of them at the end of the year. Our enslaved ancestors certainly didn't have time for appetizers; they more than likely nibbled on the sweet meat of pecans whenever they could be found. Sautéing the nuts briefly in a bit of butter just seems to bring out that sweetness.

1 pound shelled pecans   2 tablespoons unsalted butter

Pick over the pecans and remove any shells and shriveled nuts. (Just because the package claims the nuts are shelled, you shouldn't believe it. Pick over them!)

Heat the butter to foaming in a large cast-iron skillet. Add the pecans and cook them for 3 to 5 minutes, stirring them occasionally with a wooden spoon to make sure that they are well coated with butter. When they are ready, drain on absorbent paper and serve warm.

WILTED WINTER SALAD WITH JERUSALEM ARTICHOKES

•••••••••••
SERVES 8

Salads were definitely not a regular part of the diet of our ancestors, but they did pick wild greens and eat them in various ways. Jerusalem artichokes, tubers that grow underground, were there for the finding, and were a special treat.

This salad could be made from any hearty wild greens that might be available; it can also be prepared from a mix of watercress and dandelion greens. The dressing uses bacon, but if your family does not eat pork, you can use beef bacon.

½ pound Jerusalem artichokes
1 bunch watercress
1 bunch dandelion greens
1 small red onion, sliced
4 strips pork or beef bacon, cut into
   1-inch strips

2 tablespoons cider vinegar
1 teaspoon molasses
1 tablespoon water
Salt and freshly ground black pepper,
   to taste

Bring 2 cups of water to a boil in a medium-sized saucepan. Wash the Jerusalem artichokes, scrubbing them well to remove any dirt. Place them in the boiling water, cover, and cook for 15 minutes, or until firm but fork-tender. (Cooking time will depend on the size of the individual artichokes, so check occasionally. They may not all be done at the same time.)

While the artichokes are cooking, wash the salad greens, discarding any yellowed or blemished ones. Place the greens in a glass salad bowl with the onion slices. When the artichokes are done, peel them, cut them into thin slices, and add them to the salad bowl.

Cook the bacon until crisp in a small cast-iron skillet. When bacon is done, remove it to paper towels and pour off all but 1 tablespoon of the rendered fat. Return the skillet to the stove over low heat. Rapidly add the cider vinegar, molasses, and water, and stir well to mix all of the ingredients. Taste and adjust the seasoning. (The flavor of the dressing will depend on the saltiness of your bacon, the tartness of your vinegar, and the brand of your molasses, so taste it.) Add the bacon to the greens, then pour the dressing over the salad and serve warm.

ROAST CHICKEN

·············
SERVES 4

A wonderful Creole proverb states, "When the preacher comes to dinner the chickens cry." Even during the dark years of our enslavement, there were occasional chicken dinners. Then the birds were usually roasted on spits in front of the hearths that were the sole source of heat and light in many of the cabins. Nothing quite tastes like hearth-roasted chicken, but this oven-roasted bird comes close. The chicken can be served in a salad, in sandwiches, or served cold with one of the chutneys from the book (see pages 42, 99, and 145).

1 chicken (3⅓ to 4 pounds)
3 tablespoons butter
1 medium-sized onion
1 tablespoon Bell's or other poultry
  seasoning

Salt and freshly ground black pepper,
  to taste

Preheat the oven to 450 degrees. Remove the bag of giblets from the cavity of the chicken and wash the bird thoroughly inside and out. Pat it dry.

Place half of the butter in a small saucepan and melt it. Cut the remaining half of the butter into small pieces. Insert the butter pieces under the breast and leg skin of the chicken to keep it tender.

Rub the onion with the melted butter and place it in the cavity of the chicken. Rub the remaining butter, melted and unmelted, all over the chicken. Prepare a mixture of the seasonings and rub them over the chicken as well.

Place the chicken in a baking pan and into the oven. After 15 minutes, lower the heat to 350 degrees and roast, checking it occasionally, for 1 hour and 15 minutes, or until the chicken juices run clear when pricked with a fork at the leg joint. Serve hot.

SPICY VINEGAR

•••••••••••••••••••
MAKES 1 PINT

This easy-to-prepare hot vinegar not only adds a bit of taste to any soup or to mixed greens, it is also a wonderful gift for friends who cook. You will need a decorative pint bottle, scalded, and a cork. You can scald the bottle by running it through the dishwasher.

1 carrot, scraped
1 small (½-inch) piece of fresh
   ginger
4 branches fresh thyme
3 cloves garlic

1 small piece habanero or other hot
   chile, or to taste
1 pint cider vinegar

Cut the carrot into thin strips and place them in the bottle. Force the remaining ingredients into the bottle, add the vinegar, and cork. Allow the vinegar to stand for one week and then use as you wish. The intensity of the chile will increase over time.

BAKED SWEET POTATOES

••••••••••••
SERVES 8

Traditionally, while the dinner chicken was roasting on the spit, the sweet potatoes were slow-cooking in the ashes of the fire. Simply baking sweet potatoes somehow brings out all of their sweetness. Look for the smaller ones—they're sweeter; and remember, even if they call them yams, they're not. (Yams are something else all together!)

8 medium-sized sweet potatoes   2 tablespoons olive oil

Scrub the sweet potatoes well (after all, they're grown in the ground and you don't want to eat dirt). Prick them with a fork, rub them with the olive oil, and place them in the oven with the chicken. If you want to prepare the potatoes without the chicken, it takes about 1 hour in a 375-degree oven to bake them.

HOME-STYLE COLLARDS WITH SPICY VINEGAR

SERVES 6

I am fanatic about greens and I prefer collard greens to all others. The recipe is for collards, but you can use whatever greens, like kale or mustard, that you like. Winter is the best time for all greens; some say they only taste their best after they're hit by the first frost. When shopping for greens, select the youngest leaves. They will be the most tender; naturally, avoid any yellow or blemished ones.

4 pounds young, leafy collard greens
4 strips bacon
1 small ham hock*
6 cups water

Salt and freshly ground black pepper, to taste
1 onion, minced, as condiment
1 cruet Spicy Vinegar (page 119)

Place the greens in a sinkful of cold water and wash them thoroughly. Cut out any discolored spots and the fibrous central stem on all but the smallest leaves.

Render the fat from the bacon in the bottom of a large, heavy stockpot. Add the greens, ham hock or other smoked meat, and the water and bring to a boil; then lower the heat and cook for 2 hours or longer, adding water if necessary. The greens are ready when the meat of the ham hock falls off the bone and the greens are tender. Season and serve.

Don't discard the liquid in which they cooked. That's the "pot likker" and is served with the greens and savored like soup. Obligatory table condiments include a small bowl of chopped onions and spicy vinegar.

*You may subsititute a piece of smoked chicken, beef, or turkey, if you prefer.

HOLIDAY GINGERBREAD
WITH MOLASSES WHIPPED CREAM

SERVES 8

*Gingerbread was a special-occasion treat for many of our ances-
tors. The molasses was usually available and the spices were either
received as gifts or "liberated" from the Big House kitchen.*

1 tablespoon butter for greasing
  baking pan
1 cup dark molasses
½ cup boiling water
2¼ cups flour
1 teaspoon baking soda

½ teaspoon powdered cinnamon
1½ teaspoons powdered ginger
½ teaspoon salt
4 tablespoons melted butter
¼ cup packed dark brown sugar
Molasses Whipped Cream (page 123)

Preheat the oven to 350 degrees. Butter an 8-inch square baking pan.

Pour the molasses into a medium-sized mixing bowl and add the
boiling water. Sift the dry ingredients into the molasses mixture.
Add the melted butter and brown sugar and beat well either
manually or with an electric mixer.

Pour the batter into the prepared pan and place in the oven. Bake
for 35 minutes, or until a toothpick inserted in the middle comes
out clean. Serve with molasses whipped cream.

MOLASSES WHIPPED CREAM

MAKES ABOUT 2 CUPS

This is a simple way with whipped cream that adds a little something to anything it goes with.

½ pint heavy whipping cream 3 tablespoons dark molasses

 Place the whipping cream in a medium-sized bowl and begin to whip it with a wire whisk, slowly drizzling the molasses into the cream. Alternatively you can do the same with an electric mixer. When the cream is whipped into firm peaks, drop it by the spoonful onto the gingerbread and serve.

EGGNOG

•••••••••••
SERVES 6

This version of the classic holiday drink is a nonalcoholic one that can be savored by young and old alike. This eggnog is superrich and not for the dieter or the lactose intolerant. If there are concerns about salmonella-contaminated eggs in your area, use a commercially processed eggnog instead. For a more adult version, add brandy, rum, sherry, or port to taste.

5 eggs, separated
¼ cup packed light brown sugar
3 cups chilled half-and-half
1 cup chilled milk
1 teaspoon vanilla extract

⅛ teaspoon freshly grated nutmeg, plus additional for garnish
Pinch powdered cinnamon
¼ cup granulated sugar
Brandy, rum, sherry, or port to taste

Beat the egg yolks and the light brown sugar together in a medium-sized bowl. Slowly add the half-and-half, milk, vanilla, nutmeg, and cinnamon and whip until the mixture becomes foamy.

With a mixer or a whisk, beat the granulated sugar and the egg whites in an unlined copper bowl until they form soft peaks. Slowly fold the egg whites into the milk mixture. Cover the eggnog and chill it until ready to serve. Add the alcohol of choice, if you wish.

The eggnog is traditionally served in small glass punch cups and is spiced up with the addition of a grinding of fresh nutmeg on the top of each cup.

PROJECT

Starting out with a goal and accomplishing it is a thrill for all of us. It's actually one of the things that makes cooking so much fun: You get to see the end product of your labor in a reasonable amount of time and you get to enjoy it with family and friends. Setting goals and accomplishing them is one thing that gives us all a sense of purpose.

The project for this, the fifth night of Kwanzaa, is a cooking project that can be done by the whole family: the preparation of gift bottles of spicy vinegar to be given to family and friends. You can use fancy decorative bottles that can be purchased at discount stores, or recycle wine or other attractive household bottles that have been scruplously cleaned and scalded. The recipe for the spicy vinegar that appears on page 119 is simple and all hands in the household can participate. It is easily expanded: simply purchase a gallon jug of inexpensive vinegar, get more of the other ingredients, and go to it. Even if children of the house are too small to wield a knife, they can scrape carrots, peel garlic, or simply stuff the carrot pieces into the narrow bottle necks with their tiny fingers.

When the vinegar is finished, think of ways to decorate the bottles. Hardware stores and gourmet shops sell corks, and the season makes finding things like ribbon and fancy twine a snap. You may even wish to finish the bottle off with sealing wax and a handwritten label. You set a goal. You worked toward it. You attained it. Enjoy it. That's what *Nia* is all about.

FAMILY PAGE

TO DO ALWAYS AS MUCH AS WE CAN, IN THE WAY WE CAN,

MORE BEAUTIFUL AND BENEFICIAL THAN WE INHERITED IT.

THE SIXTH NIGHT

KUUMBA

CREATIVITY

The KARAMU Feast
An African-American Healing Supper

Do well today on account of tomorrow. —*Traditional saying*

At old revival meetings, preachers would lean over the pulpit and holler, "We need a healing here tonight." Indeed, in our communities, in our families, in our relationships, and in ourselves, we need a healing. I've taken the sixth night of Kwanzaa, the night of *Kuumba* or creativity, to attempt to begin that process with a communal meal that opens the gates of remembrance through food and speaks of our history, our past, and our hopes for the future. I call it a healing supper. It can be moved to any night of Kwanzaa, or indeed to any other time of the year that you, your family, or your community feels the need for a healing. The healing supper will take us back over the centuries in remembrance of our journey that began in sorrow and ends with a vision of a new day. We can do this seated around our tables at home or away.

Our tables have traditionally been among our preferred places for communion, so what better place to begin the healing process? At our tables, generations speak with each other over platters of fried chicken and bowls of potato salad. Crisis-torn families are slowly knit back together while savoring slow-cooked string beans and munching on cornbread. Dishes are passed, conversation begins, and a healing takes place. We need that healing now. Whether in a small family gathering around a simple scarred kitchen table that has served generations or in a community-wide celebration complete with drummers and dignitaries, elders, and honored guests, the feast of *Karamu* that marks the sixth day of the holiday is the ideal time for us to come together to begin to take steps to heal ourselves

In preparing the table and the foods for the *Karamu* healing supper, the principles of *Ujamaa* and *Kuumba* should be uppermost. Make a vow to try to use African-American purveyors. You don't have to spend a lot of money, but when you do spend, spread your cash around among the folk. Seek out specialty merchants who sell African fabric for use as tablecloths. Think of using a Gullah basket or other representation of our creativity for your centerpiece. You may want to splurge on a dish or two from a local potter. Be inventive. Be creative. Be expressive. Be yourself. Make the table itself a celebration of your family and its creativity.

During the healing supper, the table is set with plates and silverware for the assembled guests. The *kikombe cha Umoja* or communal chalice is set at the place of the elder who will lead the ceremony. After libation is poured, it is passed around to those assembled. At each place, there should be a glass for wine, fruit juice, or molasses water, so that each guest will have a glass for the four libation sips that follow the reading of the opening statement and with which to propose toasts and offer humorous interventions throughout the meal. The healing supper is about the celebration of how we got here, how we survived, and where we're going. Table conversation, toasts, and comments should be a way to share experiences, share the pains, share the laughter, share the joy. Tall tales, family stories, and jokes all have their place. They are all a part of our communal oral tradition. While this is not the time for "The Signifying Monkey," it is the time to remember, to retell, and to reminisce.

In addition to standard table settings, somewhere on the table there should be small bowls of the gel from the aloe plant, molasses, and sesame, as they will be referred to during the healing supper. When each is mentioned, the small bowl is passed and each guest dips in a finger to taste. An extra place is set symbolically at the communal table, with a plate of food, for all of those who went before whose names we do not know.

If possible, all of the guests should sit at one table. No "children's tables," please. The children are part of the reason for the healing supper and, with the elders, are important and honored guests.

KWANZAA STATEMENT

As on all other nights of the holiday, the ceremony begins with the Kwanzaa question *Habari gani?* Tonight's response is *Kuumba.* The response is followed by the lighting of the Kwanzaa candles on the *kinara,* tonight the last red candle, that of *Kuumba,* or creativity. All should stand as a sign of respect during the lighting of the candles and the pouring of libation. At the beginning of the meal, libation is poured and the names of the known deceased members of the host family are called while an elder who has been selected to lead the group says:

Light, peace, progress, and evolution to the ancestors of the
_____ family.

Light, peace, progress, and evolution to the ancestors of those assembled here.

Light, peace, progress, and evolution to the ancestors of all people of color throughout the world.

Light, peace, progress, and evolution to those who symbolize the principle of KUUMBA, creativity, particularly to those spirits from Africa and this hemisphere who kept us keepin' on with their stories and songs, their music and laughter, their dance, design, and dedication.

Tonight and all nights of the year, we celebrate the artistry of our people: the GRIOTS and the bricklayers, the office workers and opera singers, cooks and carpenters, poets and politicians, inventors and quiltmakers, doctors, deacons, and dressmakers—in short all of those who with their inventiveness and their creativity enabled us to survive by daily making our communities, and indeed the larger community of the world, a better and more beautiful place.

OPENING HEALING SUPPER STATEMENT

After the candles have been lighted, libation has been poured, and all have been seated, the youngest person present begins the Healing Ceremony.

Youngest Person: If we forget our past, we will be doomed to repeat it.

Elder: From too much sleeping we have forgotten.

All: We awaken to the knowledge of the past and the promise of the future. We awaken and we remember. (All take a sip from their glasses.)

Elder: We are the descendants of the peoples of Africa. The grasslands and the forest, the Sahel and the seashore come together in us.

All: We salute our African past. (Sip from glasses.)

Elder: We are the descendants of the peoples of the Americas: Creek and Cherokee, Seminole and Wampanoag, Choctaw and Sioux come together in us. Even if we do not have their blood in our veins, we walk on their land, and so we honor them.

All: We salute our Native American past. (Sip from glasses.)

Elder: We are children of a new place. Never before in the history of the world have there been any like us. The blood of all nations is in us. We cover north, south, east, and west, black, red, yellow, and white. The blood of the world runs in us.

All: We salute our international past. (Sip from glasses.)

Elder: Tonight, as we sit around this table and share this meal, we take a journey back over time and space. We take this journey to trace and remember one made by our ancestors who were brought to this land. It is a journey that begins in sorrow and ends this evening with the vision of a new day. We take this journey to link us with our past. We take this journey to remember, so that all of us seated at this table and all tables like this will know our past and remember, so that we can determine our future. We take this symbolic journey tonight so that in the future we will all truly be free.

Following the preliminary statement, the food is passed. Food is served family style. Elders should help youngsters and all should help those who can't help themselves, symbolizing the need to aid each other within our communities.

The appetizer course is pickled black-eyed peas. As the dish is passed, the first honored guest reads.

Guest #1: In the beginning, we were African: Wolof and Tutsi, Mandinka and Hausa, Ewe and Yoruba, Ashanti and Kikuyu. In our African homelands, we ate many things. We eat black-eyed peas tonight to remind us of the peas and beans that we ate in that other place. We eat them for luck and for wisdom and to remind us where we are from.

After the course is finished, there is a minute of silence, after which the first honored guest continues to read.

Guest #1: We were captured and taken against our will, sent forth from ports like Gorée and Kormantine, Ouidah and Elmina, Calabar, and Cape Coast. Our names were taken from us, our heritage mocked, our strength survived.

All: We honor the survival of our ancestors.

The fish course is served. As the dish is passed, the next honored guest reads.

Guest #2: The water deep. The water wide. The water profound. There is mystery in the water. There is another Africa at the bottom of the ocean peopled with the spirits of those who did not survive the journey. Others used water to take us away from our home and it is the water that will take us back home. We salute the water mother that is the source of all life. She gives us her fish to eat. We eat them and rejoice, knowing that she helped us survive. Tonight we eat fish as a symbol of our survival.

After the course is finished, there is a minute of silence, during which the second honored guest reads.

Guest #2: *The spirits of those who live under the water guide us and heal us. Help us to honor the sacrifice you made in everything we do. (The small bowl with aloe gel is passed and all guests dip in a finger and taste the bitterness.) We taste the bitter aloe from our African home to remind us of the trials of our ancestors.*

All: *We remember the African homeland of our ancestors.*

The turkey with heritage stuffing is served. As the dish is served, the cook who prepared the turkey reads.

Cook: *We were brought to another land. In this new land, we met new foods. Among these foods was turkey. The way we prepare a turkey speaks to who we are. Recipes for stuffings are handed down in families and are a part of our heritage in this land. Tonight, we eat my family's recipe for _____ stuffing. I learned it from _____ and serve it to you tonight. Eat and share with my history.*

VEGETARIAN ALTERNATIVE

Many of us are becoming vegetarian. If that is the case with your family and friends, present a vegetarian casserole at this point and have the cook discuss it saying:

Cook: *We were brought to another land. In this land we met new foods. In our family we have decided to leave behind the eating of meat and to eat in a vegetarian manner. This speaks to who we are and to who we hope our children will become. Our recipe for _____ is a family one, one that we have developed and one that we savor. I learned it from _____ and serve it to you tonight. Eat and enjoy my history.*

There should be many vegetables, but there should always be dishes of stewed okra, baked tomatoes, and white rice, as well as cornbread, as these foods will be referred to. As the okra, tomatoes, and rice are passed, the next honored guest reads.

Guest #3: We ate okra in our African Motherland. We brought it to this land. We eat okra tonight to celebrate our links with our past.
We eat tomatoes and cornbread tonight to symbolize our links with our new land and with the people who first walked here.
We eat rice tonight to symbolize the work of those who built this country, who went unheralded, unpaid, and unsung. In eating rice, we salute their genius, their work, and their strength.

The meal is served and savored. When it is over, there is a minute of silence, after which the small dish of molasses is passed around and the third honored guest reads.

Guest #3: We taste molasses tonight to symbolize the work of our ancestors in this land who built, and plowed, harvested, and created. In tasting this molasses, we honor their memory.

All: We honor the memory of our American ancestors.

The dessert is served. During the service the next guest to the right reads.

Guest #4: A life without sweetness is a life without hope. We eat this dessert tonight to remind ourselves that all life needs sweetening. We eat this dessert tonight to remind ourselves of our reasons for living, of the joys of family, of the delights of friendship, of the comforts of hearth and home, and of our sweet hopes for the generations yet to come.

All: We celebrate the sweetness of life.

At the conclusion of the meal, the fifth honored guest signals the end of the meal by passing around the small bowl of sesame seeds.

Guest #5: May the joys of all of our people be as numerous as the seeds in this bowl. May we grow and thrive in the year to come. May we honor the principles of the Nguzo Saba throughout the year as we do throughout Kwanzaa, and may we work together to heal, unite, and advance ourselves.

All: May we work together to heal, unite, and advance ourselves.

The Karamu Feast—An African-American Healing Supper

Appetizer

PICKLED BLACK-EYED PEAS

Fish Course

BIOKOSSO

Main Dish

TURKEY WITH HERITAGE STUFFING

OR VEGETARIAN CASSEROLE

Vegetables

STEWED OKRA

BAKED TOMATOES

PLAIN WHITE RICE (PAGE 63)

Bread

HERBED CORNBREAD

Condiment

SPICY CRANBERRY CHUTNEY

Salad

RED LEAF LETTUCE WITH CLEMENTINES

Dessert

KILLER PECAN PIE WITH MOLASSES WHIPPED CREAM

Beverage

RUM, WINE, FRUIT JUICE, OR MOLASSES WATER

PICKLED BLACK-EYED PEAS

·············
SERVES 8

Black-eyed peas are a part of our African legacy. In this recipe they are marinated with vinegar and hot chile to create a savory dish that is also known as Texas caviar. The black-eyed peas can be eaten as a condiment or a side dish. Here, they are served in a lettuce cup as an appetizer. To save time during the busy holiday, this recipe calls for canned black-eyed peas, though the dish can also be made with fresh or frozen peas. It. takes on a festive air with the addition of dark purple, red, and green bell pepper. Note that the black-eyed peas must marinate overnight.

2 cans (1 pound each) black-eyed peas, drained
¼ cup minced dark purple bell pepper
¼ cup minced red bell pepper
¼ cup minced green bell pepper
1 tablespoon finely minced garlic

1 small onion, minced
2 tablespoons red wine vinegar
1 tablespoon basalmic vinegar
⅓ cup olive oil
2 branches fresh thyme, crumbled
1 head Boston lettuce, separated into 8 leaves

Pour the drained black-eyed peas into a medium-sized bowl and add the bell peppers, garlic, and onion. In another bowl, combine the vinegars, olive oil, and thyme to form the marinade. Pour the marinade over the black-eyed pea mixture, cover with plastic wrap, and refrigerate overnight so that the flavors blend, stirring occasionally.

When ready to serve, place the lettuce leaves on individual plates, spoon the black-eyed peas onto the lettuce, and serve.

BIOKOSSO

•••••••••••
SERVES 8

This dish comes from the southern Côte d'Ivoire, where a version is prepared using a banana leaf wrapper. Here aluminum foil provides a reliable and readily available substitute. Select evenly sized small fish so that they will all cook in the same amount of time.

7 large, ripe, firm tomatoes, peeled, seeded, and coarsely chopped
2 large onions, chopped
2 cloves garlic, chopped
2 teaspoons fresh lemon juice
Salt and freshly ground black pepper, to taste

1 teaspoon minced habanero or other hot chile, to taste
8 medium-sized butterfish or small snappers, scaled and gutted, with heads left on

Place the tomatoes, onions, garlic, lemon juice, salt, pepper, and chile in the bowl of a food processor or blender and pulse until the mixture is transformed into a thick, coarse paste. Tear off 8 sheets of aluminum foil large enough to cover the fish. Dab a heaping spoonful of the paste onto the foil, add the fish, then an additional heaping spoonful of the paste. Close the foil into a packet and crimp it shut with your fingers. Proceed with the rest of the fish in the same manner. Preheat the broiler.

When ready, place the packets of foil on the broiler rack and grill them for 10 minutes, or until the fish is cooked. Serve warm in the packets. Guests will unfold the foil on their plates.

TURKEY WITH HERITAGE STUFFING

························

These pages are blank so that you can write down your family recipe for turkey and stuffing or your vegetarian specialty. If you're not sure, ask your mama, grandma, aunt, or great aunt—let's not be chauvinistic; ask your dad, your granddad, and your uncles as well.

No family recipe? That's too bad, but here's the place to start a tradition. Ask around. Check the papers, the magazines, and the cookbooks, and find an appealing recipe for turkey and stuffing or a vegetarian casserole. (They aren't hard to find at this time of year.) Try it, and if you truly love it and think it passes the audition, write it in after the holidays. (Don't hurry, give it time to take on some of your additions and subtractions.) Then start your own tradition.

FAMILY RECIPE

FAMILY RECIPE

STEWED OKRA

●●●●●●●●●●●
SERVES 8

Many folks just don't seem to like okra. However, the green pod that is a relative of both cotton and the hibiscus is a part of our culinary history. By now, it's no secret that okra originated in Africa, and most of the more inventive recipes using it come from the African diaspora, where it turns up fried, boiled, steamed, sautéed, in soups and in salads. This dish is for purists. The smallest, most tender okra pods are cooked until done in a bit of water. A dash of lemon juice is added at the last minute to cut some of the "sliminess" that offends some people.

2 pounds small okra pods   2 teaspoons fresh lemon juice
2 cups water

Wash the okra and pick over it, discarding any soft or blemished pods. Cut off the fibrous stem ends. Bring the water to a boil in a medium-sized saucepan. When the water has reached a rolling boil, add the okra. Lower the heat, cover, and cook until the okra is firm but fork-tender, about 5 to 6 minutes. Add the lemon juice for the last 2 minutes of cooking time, then remove from the heat, drain, and serve warm.

BAKED TOMATOES

••••••••••••
SERVES 8

Tomatoes are one of the food gifts that this hemisphere gave to the world. They traveled from the Americas to Africa, where they became a treasured part of the continent's cooking. Interestingly, there is some discussion that tomatoes might have finally reached the northeastern United States via people of African descent from the Caribbean. Wherever and however they originated, they're a welcome addition. Here they're simply cored, seasoned, and baked along with the turkey. If you're doing a vegetarian meal, just cook them in a baking dish.

8 large, ripe, firm tomatoes	Salt and freshly ground black pepper, to taste

These baked tomatoes would take 20 minutes if you were cooking them by themselves. However, as you are cooking them while the turkey is roasting, add them in the last 20 minutes of cooking. To prepare them, core the tomatoes and sprinkle them with salt and freshly ground black pepper. (You might want to add some of the herbs and seasonings that go into your turkey stuffing, so that the tastes will harmonize.) Place the tomatoes in a baking dish or around the turkey pan where they can absorb the drippings. Cook until soft and juicy.

HERBED CORNBREAD

MAKES ABOUT 12 PIECES

Like tomatoes, corn and cornmeal are new additions to the traditional African diet. However, they are additions that have been so gleefully adopted that it is virtually impossible to think of the cooking of the African Atlantic world without them. This cornbread uses canned corn (let's be realistic about what most fresh corn tastes like at this time of the year), a hint of jalapeño chiles, and a bit of thyme for seasoning.

¾ cup yellow cornmeal
¾ cup flour
2 tablespoons sugar
1 tablespoon baking powder
½ teaspoon salt
1 teaspoon dried thyme, crumbled
¾ cup milk

2 teaspoons minced preserved jalapeño or other hot chile, to taste
1 egg
3 tablespoons melted butter
2 tablespoons drained canned corn kernels

Preheat the oven to 425 degrees. Grease an 8-inch square baking pan. Sift the dry ingredients into a large bowl. Add the thyme, milk, chile, egg, and melted butter and beat for 1 minute or stir until the mixture is smooth. Add the corn, stirring well to make sure that the pieces are well distributed throughout the batter.

Pour the batter into the prepared pan, place it in the oven, and bake for 20 minutes, or until the top is lightly browned and a toothpick comes out clean when inserted into the middle. Serve hot.

SPICY CRANBERRY CHUTNEY

MAKES 1½ CUPS

Cranberry sauce of some kind just seems to be a must with turkey and stuffing. However, the whole cranberry or jellied sauce that comes in a can sometimes just doesn't have enough zing to set off a well-cooked turkey properly and to complement the well-seasoned tastes of our food. Here, then, is a cranberry chutney that I've been playing around with for over ten years. I've finally got it to the point where it's quite good and tastes just great with my mom's turkey with cornmeal stuffing. See if it works as well with your turkey and heritage stuffing.

1½ cups fresh cranberries*
1 (1-inch) piece fresh ginger, scraped
1 clove garlic, minced
2 teaspoons minced orange zest

1 teaspoon minced preserved jalapeño chile, to taste
½ cup fresh lemon juice
⅓ cup sugar

Place the cranberries, ginger, garlic, orange zest, and chile in the bowl of a food processor or blender and pulse until you have a grainy paste. (You may have to add a bit of the lemon juice to get it going.) Spoon the mixture into a medium-sized, nonreactive saucepan. Add the lemon juice and sugar, stirring well to make sure that all of the ingredients are evenly distributed. Bring to a boil over medium heat, then lower the heat and continue to cook, stirring occasionally, for about 25 minutes or until the chutney reaches a jamlike consistency. Stir all the way to the bottom of the saucepan to be sure that the mixture is not sticking to the bottom and scorching.

The chutney can be prepared a week or so ahead, in which case, pour it into a scalded jar and refrigerate until ready to use. If making it the same day, allow it to cool to room temperature and spoon it into a serving dish.

*Cranberries can be frozen and used straight from the freezer.

RED LEAF LETTUCE WITH CLEMENTINES

••••••••••••
SERVES 8

Clementines are small tangerinelike fruit that are available during the holiday season. The ones from Morocco are slightly tarter than the ones from Spain, and just perfect for this salad. Their juice turns up in the dressing.

1 large head red leaf lettuce
6 clementines, peeled
½ cup pomegranate seeds
 (approximately 1 pomegranate)

1 teaspoon finely minced garlic
Clementine Pomegranate Dressing

Wash and clean the lettuce, discarding any blemished leaves. Dry the leaves on absorbent paper and place them in a large glass salad bowl.

With a sharp knife, remove the membrane from the clementine segments and seed them. Add the clementine segments to the salad. Add the pomegranate seeds and the minced garlic. Toss the salad and drizzle on the dressing.

CLEMENTINE POMEGRANATE DRESSING

· · · · · · · · · · · · · · · · · · · ·

1 pomegranate, peeled and seeded
3 clementines
2 tablespoons olive oil

1 teaspoon balsamic vinegar
Pinch sugar

Place the pomegranate seeds in a sieve. Place the sieve over a bowl and press the juice from the seeds with the back of a wooden spoon or a wooden potato masher. With a juicer or a reamer, juice the clementines into the bowl. Add the olive oil, vinegar, and sugar and whisk thoroughly. Taste and adjust the sesonings. Cover with plastic wrap and chill for 1 hour, then drizzle over the salad.

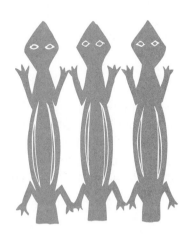

KILLER PECAN PIE WITH MOLASSES WHIPPED CREAM

•••••••••••
SERVES 8

Pecans are a part of our Southern roots. Here, with the addition of a bit of molasses and brown sugar, they are transformed into a killer pecan pie, a taste of sweetness to end the meal.

Dough for one 9-inch Basic Pie Crust
    (page 82)
 3 eggs
 ⅓ cup packed light brown sugar
 ⅓ cup granulated sugar
Pinch salt
 ⅓ cup melted butter

¾ cup dark corn syrup
¼ cup light molasses
 1 cup broken pecans
¼ cup pecan halves
 2 cups Molasses Whipped Cream
    (page 123)

Preheat the oven to 375 degrees. Roll out the pie dough and fit it into a 9-inch pie plate, fluting the edges. Cover the center of the pie shell with a sheet of aluminum foil, weight it with dried peas or beans, and bake it for 15 minutes or until set.

In a medium-sized bowl, briskly stir the eggs, sugars, salt, butter, corn syrup, and molasses until they are well mixed. Stir in the broken pecans.

Remove the foil and the beans from the pie shell and arrange the pecan halves in the bottom of the shell. Carefully pour the egg mixture into the pie shell. Place in the oven and bake for 45 minutes or until the pastry is golden brown and the filling is set. Serve warm, topped with molasses whipped cream.

MOLASSES WATER

MAKES 1 QUART

During the period of many of our ancestors' American enslavement, water was their only beverage. For holidays and special occasions, they improvised, using the only sweetener that they had: molasses. I've taken liberties with history and added a sprig of fresh mint and a squeeze of fresh lemon juice.

1 quart water
½ cup dark molasses, or to taste
¼ cup fresh lemon juice

5 sprigs fresh mint
Mint sprigs and lemon slices, for garnish

Mix the water, molasses, and lemon juice together in a pitcher, stirring thoroughly to make sure that the molasses is well mixed in. Refrigerate for at least 2 hours or until well chilled.

When ready to serve, bruise the mint by pressing it against the side of your serving pitcher with the bowl of a spoon, add ice, and pour in the molasses water. Serve chilled in glasses decorated with fresh mint sprigs and thin slices of lemon for garnish.

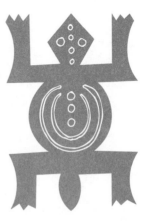

PROJECT

· · · · · · · · · · · · · · · · · · · ·

The healing supper requires that all guests know the responses to the words to be spoken during the meal. The project for this, the sixth night of Kwanzaa, the night of *Kuumba,* is to recopy the words of the healing supper ceremony on blank sheets of paper. The sheets can then be decorated with pictures of people in the African Atlantic world who represent the virtues of *Kuumba,* with designs representing the *Nguzo Saba* or with any other design that your family or organization feels is appropriate to the purpose of your healing supper. If the gathering is to be a small one, copies of the words may be individually decorated. If the gathering is a large community one, you may wish to design a different border for each page of the text and then copy them. Whichever version you decide on, remember to use the principle of *Kuumba* (creativity), to which this night is dedicated.

FAMILY PAGE

FAMILY PAGE

OUR PARENTS, OUR TEACHERS, OUR LEADERS,

TO BELIEVE WITH ALL OUR HEARTS IN OUR PEOPLE,

AND THE RIGHTEOUSNESS AND VICTORY OF OUR STRUGGLE.

THE SEVENTH NIGHT

IMANI

FAITH

The African race is like a rubber ball; the harder you knock it to the ground, the higher it will rise. —Traditional saying

On the seventh and final night of Kwanzaa, as on all other nights of the holiday, the celebration begins with the question *Habari gani?* Tonight's answer is *Imani*, or faith. The asking of the Kwanzaa question is followed by the pouring of libation from the *kikombe cha umoja* and the lighting of the candles of the *kinara*. Tonight the last candle, the green candle of *Imani*, is lighted. After the candles are lighted, thoughts turn to the spirits of those who represented the virtues of *Imani* in our communities.

Tonight is the night we celebrate the spirit of IMANI (faith).

Tonight and all other nights of the year, we celebrate the spirits of those who have gone before who represent the values of IMANI.

We celebrate the spirits of:

> Amenhotep IV of Egypt
> Agõtime of Brazil
> Bob Marley of Jamaica
> Ben Ali Mohamet of the United States
> _____ (your family selection[s])

and all those who kept their bright light of faith burning despite obstacles and odds that would have driven lesser beings to give up, give in, and give over.

Tonight and all nights, we celebrate the spirits of all of those who are here with us.

Tonight and all nights, we celebrate the spirits of those who are yet to come.

On this, the final night of Kwanzaa, we dedicate ourselves to uphold the values of IMANI and all of the principles of the NGUZO SABA. In the year that has just come in, we will have faith in the future, faith in our people, and faith in ourselves, that we may work to create a better world.

AMENHOTEP IV (AKHENATON) OF EGYPT
(PHARAOH, 1379–1362 B.C.)

Faith can move mountains, many of us were told while growing up. In ancient Egypt, Amenhotep's faith in the power of the physical sun changed the way that the world has looked at religion ever since. Was he a heretic, a religious fanatic, or a visionary. Even today, more than 3,000 years after his reign between 1379–1362 B.C., the question is still debated.

Born to kingship, Amenhotep IV ascended the throne in 1379 B.C. Physically weak and misshapen of body, he ruled surrounded by an inner circle that consisted of his mother, Queen Ti; his wife, the beautiful Queen Nefertiti; and the husband of his childhood nurse, the priest Eye. Before Amenhotep IV's reign, the priests of Amon-Re, the sun god, had attained primacy in Egypt and had become a powerful political force. Amenhotep IV would change all that. He openly challenged the priesthood and introduced the worship of Aton, the material sun, claiming that the new religion had been revealed to him; he reasoned that the sun was the source of life and heat and, through its rays, everywhere. Although other gods were tolerated, Aton became the single deity.

In witness to his devotion to the new faith, he changed his throne name from Amenhotep which means "Amon is content," to Akhenaton (Ikhnaton), meaning "It is well with Aton." He also built many temples to the new god, including one in the midst of the temple to Amon-Re. He had the names and images of Amon removed from all temples and tombs and moved the capital to Tell el Amarna, a town he called Akhetaton. Akhenaton envisioned his new god as a benificent god, one who was "father and mother of all he had made." It was revolutionary, but it was not to last.

Following the deaths of Akhenaton and Nefertiti, the old order returned, but Akhenaton's notion of one supreme universal god would live on. We salute the spirit of Akhenaton tonight as that of a visionary, one who saw beyond the day-to-day. We honor him for his courage, his insights, and for taking the first steps in establishing a concept that would change the world.

AGÕTIME OF BRAZIL
(LATE EIGHTEENTH, EARLY NINETEENTH CENTURIES)

No one is sure when Agõtime was born nor when she died. What we are sure of is that she lived. It is believed that she was born in the country of the Fongbè known as Dan Homè toward the end of the eighteenth century. She is recorded as being one of the wives of King Agoglo of Dahomey who ruled from 1789, the year of the French revolution, to 1797. When her husband died, she, unlike the childless wives who went to the grave with their husband, lived. She was passed on to Agoglo's first wife's son, Adãdozã, and went to live in the precincts of the Panther Compound of the king's wives in Abomey.

After five years in the Panther Compound, she was perceived as a threat to the king's sovereignty and sold into slavery because she was related to Gakpe, who was also a pretender to the throne. Like so many others, she last set foot on the soil of the African coast outside of the Portuguese fort of São Jão Baptista de Ajuda. She was sent to Brazil where she, with the others aboard the ship, was landed in the port city of Salvador da Bahia de Todos os Santos. Of where she went and what happened to her from there little is known, but she surfaces again, enslaved, in São Luis de Maranhão on the northern coast of the country. Legend has it that Agõtime knew she was to be taken and sent away from her African home and that her oracles told her to take her gods with her. Evidently she did, for the city of São Luis de Maranhão today is known for the religion known as *tambor de Mina*. There, and only there, the deities of the royal family of Abomey are venerated outside of Africa to this day.

The story does not end there, for in 1818, the saying, "Two suns cannot exist at the same time," was borne out. While the war drums played, Adãdozã was relieved of the crown by Gakpe, who took the king name Ghezo. He ruled for forty years. Some say that he sent emissaries to Brazil in search of Agõtime and that she was returned to glory in his kingdom. Others say she wandered off into the Brazilian forests, never to be seen again. Whatever Agõtime's fate, we salute her tonight for embodying the virtue of

Imani. Throughout her harrowing history, she never lost her faith or her Faith. She went from royalty to slave to priestess, taking her faith with her, nurturing it, and then leaving it behind as a legacy so that we would remember.

ROBERT NESTA MARLEY OF JAMAICA (1945–1981)

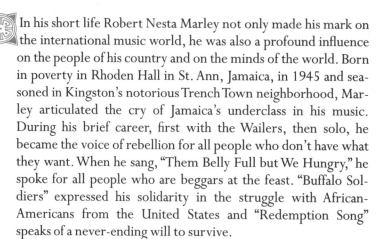

In his short life Robert Nesta Marley not only made his mark on the international music world, he was also a profound influence on the people of his country and on the minds of the world. Born in poverty in Rhoden Hall in St. Ann, Jamaica, in 1945 and seasoned in Kingston's notorious Trench Town neighborhood, Marley articulated the cry of Jamaica's underclass in his music. During his brief career, first with the Wailers, then solo, he became the voice of rebellion for all people who don't have what they want. When he sang, "Them Belly Full but We Hungry," he spoke for all people who are beggars at the feast. "Buffalo Soldiers" expressed his solidarity in the struggle with African-Americans from the United States and "Redemption Song" speaks of a never-ending will to survive.

Marley's importance, though, extends far beyond his music to his life and his personal philosophy, which was informed by his Rastafarian faith, a gentle doctrine that asks all men to live in peace. His faith in his religion and in his people made him work to ensure harmony in his country. It also helped him see beyond the conflict to the notion that all should live in peace and that the earth provides enough for all of us. We salute the spirit of Robert Nesta "Bob" Marley tonight for teaching us gentleness. We remember him for his admonition to "Get Up! Stand Up! Don't Give Up the Fight." Finally, we honor the spirit of Bob Marley tonight for bringing us joy from sorrow, music from hardship, for his "Positive Vibration," and for reminding us that where the light of faith burns bright, all things can be done.

BEN ALI MOHAMET (NINETEENTH CENTURY)

 No one knows very much about Ben Ali Mohamet, better known as Bilali Mohamet, but it is thought that he was brought to the plantation of a man named Thomas Spaulding on Sapelo Island, Georgia, from Nassau in the Bahamas. Because he is said to have spoken French, there are those who believe that before living in Nassau, he had been enslaved on one of the then-French West Indies.

Bilali Mohamet was different from the other black people of his area. In fact he distinguished himself so much that others recalled him and his ways in their oral witness to the trials of slavery. These testimonies reveal that Bilali Mohamet was a man who ate food that was prepared differently from that of the others. He prostrated himself to pray at sunup and sundown, and he wore a fezlike cap. He had many children and they too were different. They had names like Bintu, Medina, and Fatima.

Nothing much else survived about Bilali except in the memories of his descendants and those who knew him, until the Georgia State Library received a document in 1930 that was thought to be his journal, written in what seemed to be Arabic. Perplexed, they attempted to decipher the text to no avail. Finally, after the text had been taken to African Islamic scholars, a discovery was made. The work that Ben Ali Mohamet had written was his transcription of the *Risala,* a legal text written by abu Muhammed 'abdullah ben 'abi Zaid of Kairouan, the Islamic university town in what is today Tunisia. In particular, Mohamet had transcribed the introduction and sections dealing with ablutions and the call to prayer. The confusion came because, like others taken from Africa, Ben Ali Mohamet took with him only what he had stored in his mind; he had transcribed the text from memory, the memory of a young African Koranic student decades earlier. What better testimony to the power of *Imani* (faith)!

Tonight, on this final night of Kwanzaa, we salute the spirit of Ben Ali Mohamet for his unswerving faith, for his persistence and perseverance despite overwhelming odds. We salute his will to survive and to maintain his traditions. We look at his achievements, know the adversity under which he accomplished them, and learn that with faith all things are possible.

The menu celebrating IMANI is a meal focused on where we're from and where we're heading, and features thoughtful foods, foods for thought, and some classics to bring in the New Year.

Appetizer

DATES, FIGS, AND MILK

Soup

FRUIT SOUP

Salad

NORTH AFRICAN CARROT SALAD

Main Dish

RED SNAPPER FILLETS IN CREOLE COURT BOUILLON

Starch

PLAIN WHITE RICE (PAGE 63)

Vegetables

HOPPIN' JOHN AND GREENS

SOUTHERN SUCCOTASH

Dessert

CARROT CAKE

Beverage

RASPBERRY ORANGE BUBBLY

DATES, FIGS, AND MILK

•••••••••••
SERVES 8

*There is lowercase faith and capital letter Faith. This menu begins
with a minute for capital letter Faith. Many celebrants of Kwanzaa
spend the week fasting during daylight hours as a sign of their commitment to the Nguzo Saba. For them, and for the faith (both small
and capital letters) of our ancestors, this meal begins with a symbolic fast-breaking dish of dates, figs, and milk. Nibble on the fruit
and sip the milk while remembering those whose faith and Faith
brought you through.*

1 pound Medjool dates   1 quart milk *
1 pound Smyrna figs

 Arrange the dates and figs on a platter. You may wish to
add some almonds or other nuts. The platter is circulated
around the table with each diner taking a few. The milk is poured
into small glasses from a pitcher while the family thinks about
the *Nguzo Saba* of *Imani.*

*The lactose-intolerant may wish to participate with a glass of cool water.

FRUIT SOUP

∙∙∙∙∙∙∙∙∙∙∙∙

SERVES 8

This is a soup of hot winter juices that my mother dreamed up to serve as the beginning of fancy meals. Fruit soup can be prepared from fresh (I prefer fresh) or canned juices, but select the best, whichever variety you choose, because the quality of the soup will depend on the quality of the juice. You can also vary the taste by using other juices that you have available. (But be careful; apple juice will make everything else brown!)

2 cups white grape juice
2 cups purple grape juice
2 cups fresh orange juice
1 cup fresh grapefruit juice
1 cup fresh tangerine juice
1 tablespoon fresh lemon juice

1 cup water
½ teaspoon powdered cinnamon
1 teaspoon freshly grated nutmeg
8 thin orange slices and freshly
   grated nutmeg, for garnish

Combine the juices, the water, cinnamon, and 1 teaspoon nutmeg in a saucepan and heat to boiling, stirring occasionally. Ladle into soup bowls and garnish each one with a slice of orange and a grinding of fresh nutmeg.

NORTH AFRICAN CARROT SALAD

••••••••••••••••••
SERVES 6 TO 8

The light, healthy salads of North Africa remind us that in the upcoming year, vegetables should be more of a part of our lives. Here, cooked carrots are spiced with a pinch of cinnamon and confectioners' sugar and seasoned with orange juice and orange-flower water.

1½ pounds carrots, scraped
¼ cup fresh orange juice
1 tablespoon fresh lemon juice
½ teaspoon freshly ground cinnamon
1 teaspoon confectioners' sugar

1 tablespoon orange-flower water, to taste
Fresh mint sprigs, for garnish

Cut the carrots crosswise into ½-inch rounds and cook them in boiling water for 10 minutes, until they are fork-tender. While the carrots are cooking, mix the juices together and grind the cinnamon using a mortar and pestle or a coffee grinder you reserve for spices. Mix the cinnamon with the sugar.

When the carrots are cooked, drain them, place them in a glass salad bowl, and pour the juices over them. Chill them for 1 hour. When ready to serve, sprinkle them with the sugar and cinnamon mixture and drizzle the orange-flower water over them. Serve garnished with mint sprigs.

RED SNAPPER FILLETS IN CREOLE COURT BOUILLON

••••••••••••
SERVES 8

This is a variation on the redfish court bouillon that is traditionally served in many of the Black Creole homes of New Orleans at Christmastime. Here, though, instead of the entire baked fish, snapper fillets are poached in the Creole court bouillon, which is more like a Creole sauce than like the classic French court bouillon poaching liquid. You may wish to serve this as a main dish, or as an alternative main dish along with the more traditional roasts that usually appear on the New Year table.

1 tablespoon olive oil
2 tablespoons flour
1 teaspoon crushed allspice berries
1 teaspoon minced fresh thyme
1 medium-sized onion, minced
1 clove garlic, minced
1 tablespoon minced celery
2 tablespoons minced green bell
  pepper
1 tablespoon minced scallion

1 tablespoon minced fresh parsley
2 bay leaves
8 large fresh tomatoes, peeled,
  seeded, and coarsely chopped
2 cups water
½ cup dry white wine
8 ¼-pound red snapper fillets
2 tablespoons fresh lemon juice
Salt to taste
¼ teaspoon minced hot chile, to taste

Prepare a roux by heating the olive oil in a large heavy nonreactive skillet. Add the flour and cook, stirring constantly until you have a tan paste. Add the allspice, thyme, onion, garlic, celery, bell pepper, scallion, parsley, bay leaves, tomatoes, water, and wine and bring the mixture slowly to a boil, stirring occasionally. The mixture will thicken into a heavy sauce. Add the fish, lower the heat, and allow the mixture to simmer for 5 minutes or until the fish is cooked.

Remove the fish fillets and keep them on a heated platter. Add the lemon juice, salt, and chile to the sauce, stir into the mixture well, and continue to cook for 3 minutes. Taste the sauce and adjust to taste. When ready, serve over the fish fillets. Serve hot with rice.

HOPPIN' JOHN
AND GREENS

The tradition in many of our families is to eat Hoppin' John (black-eyed peas and rice) for luck and greens for folding money during the incoming year on New Year's Day. Far be it from me to tell you how to cook them. So here are some pages for you to use to write down your way with Hoppin' John and Greens. (If you don't have a recipe, check my cookbook THE WELCOME TABLE.)

FAMILY RECIPES

SOUTHERN SUCCOTASH

••••••••••••
SERVES 8

This dish of okra, corn, and tomatoes is a staple on my New Year table. It's simple to make and can even be prepared with little loss of flavor from frozen ingredients and canned tomatoes. The trick is to use a hot chile and spice it just hot enough so that your guests will say, "Ah!"

2 cups corn kernels, cut from the cob or frozen

½ pound fresh or frozen okra, topped, tailed, and cut into rounds

6 ripe, firm tomatoes, peeled seeded, and coarsely chopped, or 2½ cups chopped, seeded canned tomatoes

1 tablespoon fresh lemon juice

1 habanero or other hot chile, pricked with a fork

Salt and freshly ground black pepper, to taste

Place all the ingredients in a medium-sized saucepan and bring to a boil. Lower the heat and cook for half an hour. Remove the chile and reserve it whenever it's hot enough for your taste. Serve hot with the chile on the side for those who wish to add a bit more heat.

CARROT CAKE

••••••••••••••••••••

The whir of juicers is heard in our neighborhoods more and more. If you've ever wondered what to do with all of that pulp, try this carrot cake recipe. It's a wonderful way to use the pulp that's left over after the carrots have been juiced. If you do not have a juicer, you can use 1½ cups of grated carrot, ½ cup of grated apple, and ¾ cup of apple juice.

8 medium to large carrots, scraped	1 cup packed dark brown sugar
2 small McIntosh apples, peeled	½ cup granulated sugar
2 teaspoons baking powder	¾ cup vegetable oil
1½ cups flour	2 teaspoons vanilla
1 teaspoon freshly grated nutmeg	1 teaspoon fresh lemon juice
½ teaspoon powdered cinnamon	½ teaspoon grated lemon zest
½ teaspoon salt	¾ cup chopped walnuts
3 eggs	2 tablespoons confectioners' sugar

Preheat the oven to 350 degrees. Put the carrots and apples through a juicer. Reserve 2 cups of the mixed pulp and ¾ cup of juice.

Sift the baking powder, flour, nutmeg, cinnamon, and salt into a small bowl. In a separate bowl, beat the eggs into the brown and granulated sugars and oil and add the mixed pulp. Gradually add the dry ingredients and the reserved juice until you have a smooth batter. Stir in the vanilla, lemon juice, zest, and nuts, mixing well to make sure the nuts are evenly distributed, then pour into a greased, floured 9 x 5 x 3-inch loaf pan.

Bake for 45 minutes, or until a toothpick inserted into the middle comes out clean. Remove from the oven and allow the cake to cool in the pan before removing. Then dust with confectioners' sugar.

RASPBERRY ORANGE BUBBLY

•••••••••••
SERVES 8

The last day of Kwanzaa is a day of reflection, but it's also a day of celebration, for the first of the year always means a new beginning. Here's a celebration drink with which to toast friends and family, and with which to vow to do better and be better in the coming year. Those who do not drink alcohol can substitute ginger ale for the Champagne and have a wonderful punch.

¼ cup frozen raspberries
2 cups chilled fresh orange juice

1 bottle chilled nonvintage Champagne, sparkling wine, or ginger ale

Place the frozen raspberries in the bowl of a blender and liquefy. Gently stir the liquefied berries and the remaining ingredients together in a pitcher and serve in stemmed Champagne glasses. Toast the future and your hopes for it.

PROJECT

....

Knowledge is like a garden: if it is not cultivated,
it cannot be harvested.
—Guinean proverb

The project for this final day of Kwanzaa is one that places its emphasis on the *Nguzo Saba* of *Imani* (faith). It is one that looks ahead not only to the coming year but also to the larger future. Each individual in the family should make a promise to change one unpleasant thing about themselves and their community in the upcoming year. It may be something as small as cleaning up a room or a vow to get better grades, start that business you've been talking so much about, or just to start looking for the job that you really want. You may vow to be a better friend, to keep in better touch with family, or to try to be a kinder and more thoughtful person. It may be a vow to work with a community organization or even a vow to start one with your neighbors for the betterment of your community. You may just promise to try to learn one new thing, no matter how small, each day for the upcoming year. That's a vow we all should make. Write them down and place them in an envelope here, in this book Next year, when Kwanzaa comes again, open the envelope and recall your vows. Will you have accomplished them? What better way to end the holiday than with a promise to grow and learn.

Happy Kwanzaa
Kwanzaa yena iwe na heri

INDEX